Second Edition

Skillful 4

Listening & Speaking Student's Book

Authors: Emma Pathare and Gary Pathare
Series Consultant: Dorothy E. Zemach

	Video	Listening	Vocabulary
1 GATHERING PAGE 8 **Psychology** ➤ **Discussion:** Group work **Sociology** ➤ **Lecture:** Communities in real life	Drones and security	Practice identifying jokes and colloquial allusions Learn to adopt a critical stance to information in lectures	Practice and learn words describing working in teams
2 GAMES PAGE 26 **Sports studies** ➤ **Student discussion:** Technology in sports **Sports management** ➤ **Lecture:** Children, sports, and identity	A cycling record	Practice listening to follow the way a discussion develops Use Cornell notes when listening to lectures	Review and use phrases for getting the opportunity to speak
3 ENERGY PAGE 44 **Business** ➤ **Workplace discussion:** Managing change **Social psychology** ➤ **Group lecture:** Perspectives on the past	Old buildings, new energy	Listen to recognize allusions to external events Annotate presentation slides while listening	Learn and review words for changing situations
4 RISK PAGE 62 **Business psychology** ➤ **Student brainstorm:** Rule breakers, risk-takers **Risk management** ➤ **Guest lecture:** Managing risk	Powerchair soccer	Practice identifying consensus in group speech Listen for speculation and degree of certainty	Use and learn vocabulary describing risk and conflict
5 SPRAWL PAGE 80 **Linguistics** ➤ **Debate statements:** The spread of English **Biology** ➤ **Lecture:** An unnatural spread	A river taxi	Listen to detect and repair lapses in understanding Use extension materials to support understanding	Review and practice words for relationships

Grammar	Speaking	Study skills	Unit outcomes
Recognize and use cleft sentences	Review and improve your use of phrases to keep a discussion going	Make an action plan for personal development	Identify jokes and colloquial allusions Adopt a critical stance to information Take part in an informal debate
Learn and practice structures for expressing causality	Learn to deal with issues resulting from group work	Think about and prepare for speaking up in discussions	Listen to follow the way a discussion develops Take lecture notes using the Cornell system Prepare and conduct a group discussion to evaluate a problem
Improve and use conditional structures	Practice referring to other speakers during presentations and discussions	Reflect on the nature and dynamics of group presentations	Recognize allusions to external events Listen and annotate presentation slides Prepare and give a group presentation
Practice and learn hedging language	Use language and methods for obtaining a consensus in group discussions	Discuss the values of studying collaboratively	Identify consensus in group speech Listen for speculation and degree of certainty Conduct and contribute to a group discussion to suggest solutions
Improve your recognition and use of inversions	Prepare to draft persuasive statements and ordering arguments	Consider and discuss advice for overcoming nerves	Detect and repair lapses in understanding Support listening with extension materials Prepare and make an opening statement in a debate

	Video	Listening	Vocabulary
6 BEHAVIOR PAGE 98 **Marketing** ➤ **Interviews:** Market research **Neurolinguistics** ➤ **Lecture:** Asking the right questions	Chess and memory	Practice concurrent note-taking and listening Learn to follow abstract argumentation while listening	Use phrases for navigating from one question to another
7 EXPANSE PAGE 116 **Astronomy** ➤ **Student brainstorm:** The new space race **Geography** ➤ **Lecture:** Mapping the world	Just like on Mars	Listen to identify patterns in lectures Listen to follow discussion of mathematic or scientific problems	Use phrases to describe visuals you are referring to
8 CHANGE PAGE 134 **Management** ➤ **Staff workshop:** All change, please **Media studies** ➤ **Lecture / seminar:** The changing pace of news	A job fair	Practice your understanding of non-standard accents Listen to improve understanding of rapid, colloquial speech	Review and expand vocabulary for managing discussions
9 FLOW PAGE 152 **Culture studies** ➤ **Interviews:** The history of surfing **Oceanography** ➤ **Lecture:** Ocean problems	Sun, sea, and energy	Learn to listen and interpret idioms Practice listening and making estimates or hypotheses	Learn and use words describing conditions
10 CONFLICT PAGE 170 **Applied psychology** ➤ **Debate:** Conflict resolution—what works best? **Psychology** ➤ **Two lectures:** Role conflicts	Smash things, feel better	Listen and anticipate information to come Cope with different lecture styles while listening	Use and practice vocabulary for describing behavior

Grammar	Speaking	Study skills	Unit outcomes
Review and improve indirect questions in interviews	Review and improve techniques for conducting successful interviews	Share ways of improving your research questionnaires	Practice note-taking when listening Listen to follow abstract argumentation Conduct a case study interview
Recognize and use impersonal passive structures	Discuss ways of sharing and using visual data in spoken contributions	Improve your approach to slide presentations	Identify patterns in lectures Listen to follow scientific problems Make a presentation using visual data
Practice the use of past modals in conditionals	Review and improve preparing and asking questions	Learn to anticipate and cope with lecturers' varied approaches	Listen to contributions in non-standard accents Listen to follow rapid, colloquial speech in lectures Prepare and participate in a Q&A session
Improve your understanding of complex ordering of past events	Practice using transitions to make your presentations flow smoothly	Assess your effectiveness in presentations and talks	Listen to interpret idioms Listen to make estimates and hypotheses Prepare and deliver a presentation
Learn and practice using a range of adverbs to modify statements	Learn and practice the principles and structure of formal debates	Reflect on next steps, share ideas for progressing	Listen and anticipate information to come Deal with different lecture styles when listening Conduct a formal debate

To the student

Academic success requires so much more than memorizing facts. It takes skills. This means that a successful student can both learn and think critically.

Skillful gives you:

- Skills you need to succeed when reading and listening to academic texts
- Skills you need to succeed when writing for and speaking to different audiences
- Skills for critically examining the issues presented by a speaker or a writer
- Study skills for learning and remembering the English language and important information.

To successfully use this book, use these strategies:

Come to class prepared to learn. This means that you should show up well fed, well rested, and prepared with the proper materials. Watch the video online and look at the discussion point before starting each new unit.

Ask questions and interact. Learning a language is not passive. You need to actively participate. Help your classmates, and let them help you. It is easier to learn a language with other people.

Practice! Memorize and use new language. Use the *Skillful* online practice to develop the skills presented in the Student's Book. Review vocabulary on the review page.

Review your work. Look over the skills, grammar, and vocabulary from previous units. Study a little bit each day, not just before tests.

Be an independent learner, too. Look for opportunities to study and practice English outside of class, such as reading for pleasure and using the Internet in English. Remember that learning skills, like learning a language, takes time and practice. Be patient with yourself, but do not forget to set goals. Check your progress and be proud of your success! I hope you enjoy using *Skillful*!

Dorothy E. Zemach—Series Consultant

Opening page

Each unit starts with two opening pages. These pages get you ready to study the topic of the unit. There is a video to watch and activities to do before you start your class.

Listening lessons

In every unit, there are two listening lessons. They present two different aspects of the unit topic and help you with ideas and language for your speaking task.

Vocabulary to prepare you for the listening activities

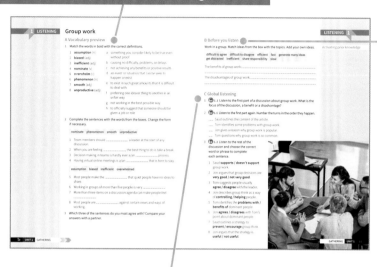

Develop your listening skills in each part of the listening lesson.

Every listening section helps you use a new listening skill.

Speaking lessons

After your listening lessons, there is a page for you to analyze a model answer to a speaking task. This will help you organize your ideas and language and prepare for your final task at the end of the unit.

First, analyze the model answer.

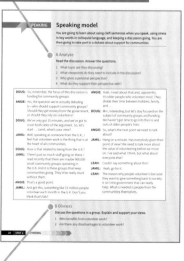

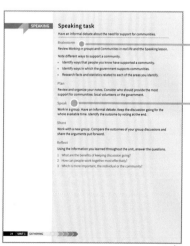

Next, discuss your ideas.

Brainstorm your speaking task and organize your ideas and language from the unit.

Finally, perform your speaking task.

Discussion point

Study the infographic about communities and answer the questions.

1 What benefits do individuals get from being with others?

2 What are the disadvantages of being in a community?

3 What causes communities to form?

4 What will happen to physical communities in the future?

5 Is *community* a positive or negative word? Why?

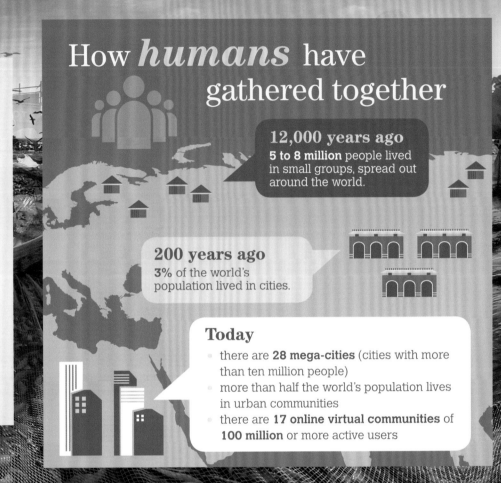

How *humans* have gathered together

12,000 years ago
5 to 8 million people lived in small groups, spread out around the world.

200 years ago
3% of the world's population lived in cities.

Today
- there are **28 mega-cities** (cities with more than ten million people)
- more than half the world's population lives in urban communities
- there are **17 online virtual communities** of **100 million** or more active users

VIDEO

DRONES AND SECURITY

Before you watch

Match the words in bold with the correct definitions.

1 **apprehend** (v)

2 **crowdsource** (v)

3 **end user** (n)

4 **nuisance** (n)

5 **plot** (v)

a someone who buys and uses a product or piece of software

b to catch

c to mark points on a graph or map

d to get ideas or help from a large number of people

e an annoying and continuing problem

LISTENING 1 Identifying jokes and colloquial allusions
LISTENING 2 Adopting a critical stance to information in lectures
STUDY SKILL Action plan for personal development

VOCABULARY Words for working in teams
GRAMMAR Cleft sentences
SPEAKING Keeping a discussion going

A fishing community gathers for a busy day.

While you watch

Watch the video and choose *T* (True) or *F* (False).

1 This video's main message is about the advantages of drones.   T / F

2 A smartphone app can be used to detect drones in the area.   T / F

3 The app can only be used by police officers.   T / F

4 The Dronewatcher app would be interesting for airports, stadiums, and gathering places.   T / F

5 Edward's company only uses one type of technology to detect drones.   T / F

After you watch

Discuss the questions in a group.

1 How many advantages of drones can you list? How many disadvantages?

2 Are there places in your area where people usually gather? What are they like?

3 Have you heard of any other good uses of crowdsourcing?

4 If you could crowdsource a problem, what would it be? Who would you ask for help?

Group work

A Vocabulary preview

1 Match the words in bold with the correct definitions.

1 **assumption** (n)	a something you consider likely to be true even without proof
2 **biased** (adj)	b causing no difficulty, problems, or delays
3 **inefficient** (adj)	c not achieving any benefits or positive results
4 **nominate** (v)	d an event or situation that can be seen to happen or exist
5 **overwhelm** (v)	e to exist in such great amounts that it is difficult to deal with
6 **phenomenon** (n)	f preferring one idea or thing to another in an unfair way
7 **smooth** (adj)	g not working in the best possible way
8 **unproductive** (adj)	h to officially suggest that someone should be given a job or role

2 Complete the sentences with the words from the boxes. Change the form if necessary.

nominate   phenomenon   smooth   unproductive

1 Team members should _____ a leader at the start of any discussion.
2 When you are feeling _____, the best thing to do is take a break.
3 Decision making in teams is hardly ever a/an _____ process.
4 Having virtual online meetings is a/an _____ that is here to stay.

assumption   biased   inefficient   overwhelmed

5 Most people make the _____ that quiet people have no ideas to share.
6 Working in groups of more than five people is very _____.
7 More than three items on a discussion agenda can make people feel _____.
8 Most people are _____ against certain views and ways of working.

3 Which three of the sentences do you most agree with? Compare your answers with a partner.

B Before you listen

Work in a group. Match ideas from the box with the topics. Add your own ideas.

difficult to agree   difficult to disagree   efficient   fast   generate many ideas
get distracted   inefficient   share responsibility   slow

The benefits of group work:_____

_____

The disadvantages of group work:_____

_____

C Global listening

1   🎧 **1.1** Listen to the first part of a discussion about group work. What is the focus of the discussion, a benefit or a disadvantage?

2   🎧 **1.1** Listen to the first part again. Number the turns in the order they happen.

___ Saud outlines the content of the article.

___ Tom identifies some problems with group work.

___ Jon gives a reason why group work is popular.

___ Tom questions why group work is so common.

3   🎧 **1.2** Listen to the rest of the discussion and choose the correct word or phrase to complete each sentence.

1   Saud **supports / doesn't support** group work.

2   Jon argues that group decisions are **very good / not very good**.

3   Tom suggests people usually **agree / disagree** with the leader.

4   Jon describes group think as a way of **controlling / helping** people.

5   Tom identifies the **problems with / benefits of** dominant people.

6   Jon **agrees / disagrees** with Tom's point about dominant people.

7   Saud outlines a strategy to **prevent / encourage** group think.

8   Jon argues that the strategy is **useful / not useful**.

Identifying jokes and colloquial allusions

D Close listening

English speakers often use humor to create a relationship with listeners. Humor is based on shared knowledge not explicitly stated. The speaker makes the assumption that the listeners will understand.

Not that we'd ever say something to please our tutor, of course! We would never do that, would we?

Colloquial allusions often use very informal language or, sometimes, language from a specific region of a country.

Yeah, a little bit like those khakis you're always wearing, Jonno!

Identifying jokes and colloquial allusions will help you to understand the speaker's view and relationship with the listeners. Observe how other listeners respond. When they find something humorous, "unpack" what was said by checking that you …

- understand all the language.
- know who or what was referred to.
- have sufficient background information.

1 🎧 **1.3** Listen to parts of the discussion again and choose the correct answers.

1 In Jon's first year of college, he **worked very hard / didn't work very hard / always worked in a group**.

2 Some of the student's tutors probably have **a strong academic background / careers in teaching history / some failed tests in their pasts**.

3 Jon shows the group **that Tom's point is correct / that he agrees with Tom / that Tom is wrong about group work**.

2 🎧 **1.4** Listen to three more extracts. What does the speaker actually think?

1 Tom   a There are lots of problems in the world.

           b We face few problems in the world today.

2 Tom   a We have agreed to things in groups that we didn't really believe.

           b We would never say things in a group that we didn't believe.

3 Jon   a We must stop people from being different.

           b We should allow people to be different.

E Critical thinking

1 Work on your own.

Student A: Make a list of the challenges of working individually.

Student B: Make a list of the challenges of working in groups.

2 Share and discuss your lists.

Study skills — Action plan for personal development

Making an action plan helps you to focus your efforts and achieve your goals. To be most effective, follow a clear procedure:

Identify the main areas for development, e.q., *gain experience of presenting to international audiences*, and then identify the specific steps you need to take to achieve your goals, e.g., *identify some forums for international student presentations*.

A key question you need to be able to answer is *How will I know when I have completed each step?* Identify measurable outcomes, e.g., *apply to at least one forum for presentations*. Set start and end dates for each step, and congratulate yourself when you have completed each one.

© Stella Cottrell (2013)

Action plan for personal development planning goals

Main things to do	Steps to take (milestones)	What indicates successful completion?	Start date	Target completion date	Done
1	a				
	b				

1 Complete the action plan with the examples from the Study skills box. Then add another possible step and indicator of success, with a realistic time frame for both steps.

2 Discuss the questions with a partner.

   1 Which areas of your academic life would you like to develop? Why? How? By when?

   2 What advice can you give your partner from your own experience and knowledge?

3 Use the ideas from your discussion to write an action plan.

Communities in real life

A Vocabulary preview

1 Match the words in bold with the correct definitions.

1 **distinct** (adj)	a no longer used because of being replaced by something more effective
2 **evaluation** (n)	b relating to one particular thing
3 **fund** (v)	c to provide money for something that costs a lot
4 **obsolete** (adj)	d a decision about quality and value, based on careful thought
5 **provider** (n)	e an organization or company that makes a service available to the public
6 **sector** (n)	f a number that represents a fact or describes a situation
7 **specifically** (adv)	g a group that is part of a larger group
8 **statistic** (n)	h separate and different in a way that is clear

2 Complete the sentences using your own ideas.

1 Using statistics shows that you …

2 … is usually the biggest provider of education.

3 Seeing yourself as part of a distinct community can …

4 The most important sector for financial support from the government is …

5 … are examples of things that, very soon, will be obsolete.

6 … should fund sports and arts organizations.

7 Evaluation is an important part of …

8 Most libraries are aimed specifically at …

3 Compare your sentences from Exercise 2 with a partner. How many of each other's ideas do you agree with?

B Before you listen

You are going to listen to a lecture about the community sector. First, discuss the questions with a partner.

1 Which of these do you have in your area?

business-advice center   childcare center   health center   library

2 Who funds them?

C Global listening

1 🎧 **1.5** In the introduction to the lecture, the lecturer asks the question: *Do we still need them in the mobile, virtual age?* Which organization do you think he is talking about? Listen and check.

2 🎧 **1.6** Listen to the rest of the lecture and number the main ideas in the order they are presented.

Listening to a sequence of arguments

___ Libraries will need to offer different services in the future.

___ Community-sector groups are different from other organizations.

___ Libraries could be places for people to gather.

___ Evidence shows that the community sector helps many people.

_2_ Has technology decreased the need for certain things?

___ There are many arguments against libraries.

_1_ The idea of communities with centers is being challenged.

___ Some people think there is no future for libraries.

Adopting a critical stance to information in lectures

D Close listening

Thinking critically about the information presented in lectures will help you to identify the argument presented, along with the reasons and evidence. You will then be able to evaluate this argument and consider alternative perspectives.

Use a series of questions to provide a framework for the critical stance, e.g.,

What is the main argument or viewpoint?
What supporting evidence is provided?
What alternative arguments or viewpoints might there be?

1 🎧 **1.7** Listen to four extracts from the talk. Match the extract with the lecturer's actions.

The lecturer ...

gives his own view with no supporting information.   ___

assumes everyone knows the same information.   ___

refers to but provides no proof of specific evidence.   ___

believes that most people have the same opinion.   ___

2 🎧 **1.7** Listen again and then discuss the questions with a partner.

1 What supporting evidence is provided?

2 What alternative arguments or viewpoints might there be?

3 🎧 **1.8** Listen to four more extracts. Identify how these arguments are supported. Match the methods (a–d) with the extract numbers (1–4).

a references on a handout ___   c quoting somebody's opinion ___

b using a statistic ___   d referring to a research study ___

E Critical thinking

1 Work in small groups. Choose one of the community-sector groups. Make a list of what the public generally wants and needs from such a group.

business-advice center   childcare center   health center   library

2 Exchange lists with another group. Identify how the community-sector group could ensure that the public is satisfied.

Critical thinking

Logical fallacy: anecdotal evidence

Arguments sometimes contain problems in their logical structure and are, therefore, less valid. One type of logically fallacious argument uses anecdotal evidence.

I know a person who …
My experience is that …

Anecdotal evidence relies on informal personal experience. One problem is that people often remember more unusual stories. They then provide these exceptions as support for an argument, though the anecdotal evidence is not supported by scientific research.

What about the case where … ?

Another problem is the assumption that if one event happens after another, the first event is the cause of the second.

So that proves it.
There has to be a connection.

1   Read the extracts from the discussion and the lecture. Identify the anecdotal evidence.

   1   What it is is that people don't trust others to work alone. They think people just won't do any work.

   2   If you put people in a group, it's always the same people who get to speak, and the quieter people can feel overwhelmed, never getting to speak … you know, like Sam? We always end up doing what he suggests, for some reason. If he told us to jump off a building, we probably would!

   3   And it isn't really true … what about last week in the tutorial when Susi had that great idea about the presentation? She never usually speaks, but everyone listened to her …

   4   … because people just won't need to go to a library to borrow books or go there to use a photocopier. I certainly won't, anyway. I access most of the articles I need for my work online, and I'm sure you do, too.

2   Work with a partner. Discuss the problem with the anecdotal evidence in each extract, and the kind of evidence that could be included to strengthen the arguments.

3   Discuss the questions in small groups.

   1   How can forms of anecdotal evidence be useful, e.g., in law or medicine?

   2   What support can be given to anecdotal evidence to make it useful?

Vocabulary development

Words for working together

1 Complete the definitions with the words in the box.

| antisocial | collaborate | membership | open to |
| participant | perspective | productivity | voluntary |

1 _____ (n) someone who takes part in something
2 _____ (v) to work with someone in order to produce something
3 _____ (n) the rate at which goods are produced or work is done
4 _____ (n) a way of thinking about something
5 _____ (n) belonging to an organization, group, or club
6 _____ (adj) not interested in meeting other people, or not enjoying friendly relationships
7 _____ (adj) done because you chose to do it, not because you have to
8 _____ (adj) willing to consider different possibilities

2 Choose the best words to complete the collocations.

1 annual **perspective / open to / membership**
2 **voluntary / collaborate / productivity** work
3 **productivity / voluntary / antisocial** behavior
4 **collaborate / open to / perspective** suggestions
5 alternative **antisocial / participant / perspective**
6 an increase in **productivity / open to / participant**
7 **voluntary / collaborate / productivity** closely with others
8 active **antisocial / participant / perspective**

3 Choose five of the collocations from Exercise 2 and explain to your partner how each one connects to your life.

For example:

I have an annual membership at a local gym.

Academic words

1 Match the words in bold with the correct definitions.

1	**conformity** (n)	a	more successful or powerful than other people of the same type
2	**deviation** (n)		
3	**dominant** (adj)	b	a feeling of being embarrassed and finding it difficult to relax or speak
4	**impose** (v)		
5	**inhibition** (n)	c	not willing to do something
6	**justification** (n)	d	to influence or control something in a clever or dishonest way
7	**manipulate** (v)		
8	**reluctant** (adj)	e	a difference in the usual or expected way of doing something
		f	to introduce something such as a new system and force people to accept it
		g	behavior that is acceptable because it is similar to everyone else's
		h	a reason why something is correct

2 Complete each sentence with a word in bold from Exercise 1. Change the form if necessary.

1 It is normal to feel a degree of _____ in new situations and to find it difficult to speak.

2 It can be difficult for quieter people to speak when there are more _____ team members.

3 An effective team leader does not _____ his or her views on others.

4 The need for a quick decision is a/an _____ for the team leader to decide without the group.

5 People are often _____ to speak if they think they are going to be criticized.

6 _____ to group rules is important for a smooth working process.

7 Good team leaders know how to _____ the team members.

8 Group work becomes difficult when there is _____ from the original aims and plan.

3 Choose the three sentences you most agree or disagree with in Exercise 2. Explain your choices to a partner.

Speaking model

You are going to learn about using cleft sentences when you speak, using stress in key words in colloquial language, and keeping a discussion going. You are then going to take part in a debate about support for communities.

A Analyze

Read the discussion. Answer the questions.

1 What topic are they discussing?
2 What viewpoints do they need to include in the discussion?
3 Who gives a personal perspective?
4 What do they support their perspective with?

DOUG: So, remember, the focus of this discussion is funding for community groups.

ANGIE: Yes, the question we're actually debating is—who should support community groups? Should they get money from the government, or should they rely on volunteers?

DOUG: We've only got 15 minutes, and we've got to cover both sides of the argument. So, let's start … Jamil, what's your view?

JAMIL: Well, speaking as someone from the U.K., I feel that volunteer work is the thing that is at the heart of all communities.

DOUG: How is that related to being from the U.K.?

JAMIL: There's just so much stuff going on there. I read recently that there are maybe 900,000 small community groups operating in the U.K. And it is these groups that keep communities going. They'd be really stuck without them.

ANGIE: That's a good point.

JAMIL: And get this, something like 15 million people volunteer each month in the U.K. Don't you think that's fab?

ANGIE: Yeah, I read about that and, apparently, it's older people who volunteer most. They divide their time between hobbies, family, and …

DOUG: Mm, interesting, but let's stay focused on the subject of community groups and funding. We haven't got time to go into the ins and outs of older people's lives.

ANGIE: So, what's the next point we need to talk about?

JAMIL: Hang on a minute. Has everybody given their point of view? We need to talk more about the value of volunteering before we move on. I've said what I think, but what about everyone else?

LEAH: Could I say something about this?

JAMIL: Yeah, go for it.

LEAH: The reason why people volunteer is because they want to give something back to society. It isn't the government that can really help. What is needed is people from the communities themselves.

B Discuss

Discuss the questions in a group. Explain and support your views.

1 Who benefits from volunteer work?
2 Are there any disadvantages to volunteer work?

Grammar

Cleft sentences

We use cleft sentences to make connections between known and new information. The information is divided into two clauses, so the focus can be on the new information.

Cleft sentences with *it*

The new information comes after *it*. The known information is in the clause after *that*. When talking about people, we can use *who*. When talking about times, we can use *when*.

It's older people who volunteer most.

Cleft sentences with *wh-* words

These sentences can use *what*, *where*, *why*, *that*, etc., or they can start with phrases such as *The reason why* … The new information can come in the first or second clause.

What is needed is people from the communities themselves.

1 Match the parts of the cleft sentences.

1		
a Volunteer work	is these groups that	is at the heart of all communities.
b It	is the thing that	keep communities going.

2		
a The reason why people volunteer	is because	can really help.
b It	isn't the government that	they want to give something back …

2 Find the cleft sentences in the model and check your answers.

3 Rewrite the following sentences as cleft sentences. Consider which information you wish to emphasize when you decide on the structure.

1 Community groups provide valuable help for local people.
2 Older people volunteer because they have more free time.
3 Participation in volunteer work can help people to develop their skills.
4 People like to collaborate to solve local problems.
5 Private donations account for community-group funding.
6 Government funding should be spent on regional and national issues.

4 Compare your sentences with a partner. How do they differ in emphasis?

Speaking skill

To explore ideas fully and make informed decisions, have a plan for your discussion and a strategy for keeping it going, even when it is informal.

1   At the start, identify the aim of the discussion and points to be discussed.
    So, as we agreed, the point of the discussion is to …
    We have four main areas to cover.

2   Ensure that everyone participates and, also, stays on topic.
    What do you think about that?
    Let's try to stay on topic.

3   Monitor the time, keep the discussion moving, and make sure everyone is ready to change topics.
    I'm afraid we'll have to leave that for another day.
    Let's move on to the next point.
    Does anyone else have anything to add to that?

4   Listen actively, respond to points made, and contribute your ideas.
    Really?
    That's a very valid point …
    If I could jump in here …

1   Match a phrase with each purpose.

    1   identify points to discuss   *What's your view?*
    2   ensure participation   *Interesting.*
    3   decide when to move on   *We have to cover both sides of the argument.*
    4   listen actively   *Has everybody given their point of view?*

2   🎧 1.9 Listen to four extracts from the model. Match each extract (1–4) with its purpose.

    ___ Identify aim
    ___ Stay on topic
    ___ Listen actively
    ___ Contribute your ideas

3   Review the model and underline the phrases the participants use to keep the discussion going.

4   Find out about your group's experience with volunteer work. Use the strategies to keep the discussion going.

Pronunciation for speaking

Stress in key words in colloquial language

Colloquial speech is often fast and may contain informal grammar and unfamiliar vocabulary. To follow this effectively, focus on the stressed words because these carry the speaker's main message.

*There's just **so much stuff** going on **there**.*

1   Match each extract with its underlying meaning.

   1   They'd be really stuck without them.
   2   And get this …
   3   Don't you think that's fab?
   4   … to go into the ins and outs of …
   5   Hang on a minute.
   6   Yeah, go for it.

   a   I think it's excellent.
   b   Wait. It's too soon to move on.
   c   Yes, you have my permission.
   d   Listen to this. It's important.
   e   They would have problems on their own.
   f   … to examine the details of …

2   🎧 1.10 Listen to the extracts above and underline the stressed words. Compare with a partner and identify the following.

   1   How does the stress help provide the meaning?
   2   What happens to the unstressed words?

3   Work with a partner. Say the sentences from Exercise 1. Aim to say them at a natural pace, with the key words stressed.

4   Review the Speaking model. Then work in groups of four, with each person taking one of the four roles from the discussion. Discuss the same topic, using some of the language from the model and focusing on using stress in the key words.

GATHERING   UNIT 1   23

Speaking task

Have an informal debate about the need for support for communities.

Brainstorm

Review *Working in groups* and *Communities in real life* and the Speaking lesson.

Note different ways to support a community.

- Identify ways that people you know have supported a community.
- Identify ways in which the government supports communities.
- Research facts and statistics related to each of the areas you identify.

Plan

Review and organize your notes. Consider who should provide the most support for communities: local volunteers or the government.

Speak

Work in a group. Have an informal debate. Keep the discussion going for the whole available time. Identify the outcome by voting at the end.

Share

Work with a new group. Compare the outcomes of your group discussions and share the arguments put forward.

Reflect

Using the information you learned throughout the unit, answer the questions.

1 What are the benefits of keeping discussion going?
2 How can people work together most effectively?
3 Which is more important, the individual or the community?

Review

Wordlist

Vocabulary preview

assumption (n) **	nominate (v) *	smooth (adj) **
biased (adj)	obsolete (adj)	specifically (adv) ***
distinct (adj) **	overwhelm (v) *	statistic (n)
evaluation (n)	phenomenon (n) **	unproductive (adj)
fund (v) ***	provider (n) *	
inefficient (adj)	sector (n) ***	

Vocabulary development

antisocial (adj)	open to (adj)	productivity (n) **
collaborate (v) *	participant (n) **	voluntary (adj) **
membership (n) ***	perspective (n) **	

Academic words

conformity (n)	impose (v) ***	manipulate (v) **
deviation (n)	inhibition (n) *	reluctant (adj) **
dominant (adj) **	justification (n) **	

Academic words review

Complete the sentences with the correct form of the words in the box.

conformity   deviation   dominant   inhibition   reluctant

1   She was able to recite the poem with no _____ from the text.
2   Bosses say they value initiative, but they're usually happy with _____.
3   Hank was _____ to leave his laboratory—he still had work to do.
4   In most groups, the person with the _____ personality normally takes the lead.
5   Basia was starving, so she loaded her plate with food with no _____.

Unit review

Listening 1	☐	I can identify jokes and colloquial allusions.
Listening 2	☐	I can adopt a critical stance to the information I hear.
Study skill	☐	I can make an action plan for personal development.
Vocabulary	☐	I can use vocabulary describing working in teams.
Grammar	☐	I can use cleft sentences.
Speaking	☐	I can keep a discussion going.

Discussion point

Study the infographic about the benefits of sports and answer the questions.

1 What additional benefits are there for each category?

2 Which category of benefits is most motivating?

3 What are the advantages for society of each of the categories of benefits?

4 Are there any negative factors in each category?

The **Benefits** of Sports

 Physical Benefits

 Psychological Benefits

 Social Benefits

Physical Benefits	Psychological Benefits	Social Benefits
› Heart disease	› Self-image	› Problem solving
› Resting heart rate	› Academic performance	› Teamwork
› BMI	› Depression	› Competition
› Blood pressure	› Well-being	› Rule following
› Life expectancy	› Learning to lose	› Leadership

VIDEO

A CYCLING RECORD

Before you watch

Match the words in bold with the correct definitions.

1 **cheer on** (v)   a to encourage

2 **former** (adj)   b previous

3 **kick the bucket** (v)   c surprising

4 **pedal** (v)   d to die

5 **remarkable** (adj)   e to power a bicycle

6 **try out** (v)   f to test

UNIT
AIMS

LISTENING 1 Following the way a discussion develops
LISTENING 2 Using Cornell notes for lectures
STUDY SKILL Speaking up

VOCABULARY Getting the opportunity to speak
GRAMMAR Expressing causality
SPEAKING Dealing with issues in group work

The start of a cycling competition.

While you watch

Watch the video and choose *T* (True) or *F* (False).

1   Robert Marchand is remarkable because he broke a cycling speed record at the age of 105.   T / F

2   Robert has broken a number of records.   T / F

3   Robert exercises regularly but only before record attempts.   T / F

4   Robert believes he could have gone faster.   T / F

5   Robert will definitely not be making any more record attempts.   T / F

After you watch

Discuss these questions in a group.

1   What would you like to ask Robert if you met him?

2   Would you like to live to 105?

3   What sports do you like to do?

4   If you could break any world record, which would it be? Why?

5   Tell the class about an old person you know.

Technology in sport

A Vocabulary preview

1 Match the words in bold with the correct definitions.

1	**elite** (n)	a	limited in what it is possible to do
2	**fundamental** (adj)	b	continuing for a long time
3	**irrelevant** (adj)	c	the possibility that something unpleasant or dangerous might happen
4	**prolonged** (adj)		
5	**restricted** (adj)	d	willing to do things that are unfair, dishonest, or illegal
6	**risk** (n)		
7	**ultimate** (adj)	e	the best or most skillful people in a group
8	**unscrupulous** (adj)	f	happening at the end of a process or activity
		g	relating to the basic nature or character of something
		h	not important for what you are discussing or doing

2 Choose the best word to complete the sentences.

1 The **irrelevant / fundamental / elite** rule of sports is to play fairly and not to cheat.

2 Medicines taken by professional sports competitors should be **ultimate / restricted / fundamental** and monitored.

3 The outcome of sports is **ultimate / irrelevant / risk**; participation is much more important.

4 Sports funding should help the general public rather than the **prolonged / elite / risk** of top athletes.

5 The world of sports is full of **unscrupulous / fundamental / prolonged** competitors who will do anything to win.

6 Winning is the **ultimate / irrelevant / unscrupulous** goal of any sports competitor.

7 To become the greatest, you must be prepared to take a **restricted / risk / elite**.

8 The human body will eventually be damaged by **fundamental / prolonged / restricted** sports training.

3 Which of the sentences do you agree with? Compare your answers with a partner.

B Before you listen

Work in a group. Which of the people listed have a role in the success of an individual sports competitor? How? How much?

- The sports competitor
- His or her family
- The sports equipment company
- The sports doctor
- The competitor's trainer

C Global listening

1  2.1 Listen to the start of a discussion about sports. What do you think the overall theme of the discussion will be?

a fairness in sports

b funding of sports

c children and sports

2 2.2 Listen to the rest of the discussion and number the main ideas discussed in order.

___ Changes in sports equipment affect past sports people as well as current sports people.

___ Some argue that doping should be made legal.

_1_ Companies are using advanced technology to develop sports equipment.

___ Separate sports events for clean athletes and dopers wouldn't solve the problem.

___ Cycling is an example of a sport dealing with more than one issue.

___ Doping can be very difficult to prove due to new developments.

___ Not everyone can use advanced sports equipment, and this is not fair.

___ Sports can be dangerous for a variety of reasons.

GLOSSARY

disgrace (v) to harm the reputation of a person by doing something bad

drag (n) the force that slows something down when it moves through air or liquid

life expectancy (n) the length of time that someone is likely to live

Following the way a
discussion develops

D Close listening

> Discussions develop in a variety of ways, often not following one particular path. However, discussions do tend to have key identifiable interactions, e.g.:
>
> Challenging a view   *"I'd like to challenge that point."*
>
> These interactions have no fixed order and can be repeated as the discussion develops. Identifying them will help you to follow the development of the discussion and understand the points made. Some of these interactions include:
>
> Establishing roles   *"I'll take notes, and you chair the discussion."*
> Introducing a topic   *"Let's begin with the question of sports events."*
> Interrupting   *"It's very important that—"*
>   *"—But what about the idea of fairness?"*
> Broadening the topic   *"Let's bring in the idea of equality, too."*

1 🎧 **2.3** Listen to the start of the discussion again. Which two interactions from the box do you hear?

> Challenging a view   Establishing roles   Interrupting   Introducing a topic

2 🎧 **2.4** Listen to parts of the discussion again and identify the interaction from the list.

Extracts 1–5

A Broadening the topic   ___
B Challenging a view   ___
C Establishing both sides of
  an argument   *1*
D Exploring with a further
  question   ___
E Interrupting   ___

Extracts 6–10

F Getting back on topic   ___
G Providing historical
  evidence   ___
H Referring to source material ___
I Speculating on future
  outcomes   ___
J Agreeing with a point   ___

E Critical thinking

Which of these views from the discussion do you agree with?

1 Unequal access to advanced sports equipment is unfair.
2 Doping cannot be stopped. Therefore, it should be accepted.
3 People should be able to decide whether to participate in risky sports.

Study skills Speaking up

Effective group work involves everyone in the group. Each group member needs to contribute and help other people to contribute.

We can help others by, e.g., asking questions, supporting views, and asking for examples.

We can help ourselves at three different stages.

Before the group work

- Make the decision to speak at least once.
- Prepare for the discussion by doing research and making notes.

During the group work

- Focus on being clear and brief.
- Give an example to support your point.
- Avoid speaking too fast and speak so everyone can hear you.
- Act confident even if you don't feel it.

After the group work

- Reflect on your contribution.
- Decide what you will do better next time.

© Stella Cottrell (2013)

1 You are going to work in a group. First, review the task.

Extreme sports, where there is a risk of injury, should not be marketed to children or young people. What do you think? Discuss the issue in a group. Then, take a final vote.

2 Check any words or concepts you don't know in the task instructions. Make notes on any ideas you may want to include in the discussion.

3 Work in a group to have the discussion.

- Speak clearly.
- Give examples.
- Ask questions.
- Show your agreement with others' views.

4 Reflect on the group discussion using the checklist from Exercise 3.

- Which things on the list did you do?
- How often?
- How effectively?
- What did other group members do well?

5 Decide what you will do differently. Discuss your decision with a partner.

Children, sports, and identity

A Vocabulary preview

1 Match the words from the box with the correct definitions.

| eliminate | enhance | initiative | interfere |
| motivate | outrage | prestige | protective |

1 _____ to encourage someone to behave in a particular way

2 _____ to deliberately become involved in a situation to try to influence it

3 _____ a strong feeling of anger and shock at something you feel is unfair

4 _____ the high reputation that someone or something has earned

5 _____ wanting to stop someone or something from being hurt

6 _____ the ability to decide in an independent way what to do and when

7 _____ to get rid of something that is not wanted or needed

8 _____ to improve something or make it more attractive or valuable

2 Complete the sentences with the words in bold from Exercise 1.

1 All competitors would _____ their sports performances if they had the opportunity.

2 It would be impossible to _____ all elements of competition from society.

3 Most sports competitors will do anything for the _____ of winning.

4 Parents and teachers should not _____ in children's playground games.

5 Parents should avoid being too _____ of their children in team sports.

6 Prize money is the most effective way to _____ sports competitors.

7 The government should take the _____ to fund more public sports centers.

8 We are right to feel _____ when a sports competitor is revealed as a cheat.

3 Identify four sentences you feel strongly about. Share the sentences and your views with a partner.

B Before you listen

You are going to listen to a lecture about children and sports. Work in a group and brainstorm a list of possible problems the lecturer could focus on.

C Global listening

1   🎧 **2.5** Listen to the start of *Children, sports, and identity*. What problem is the focus of the lecture?

2   🎧 **2.6** Listen to the rest of the lecture and number the main points in the order they are presented. (Two of the ideas are not in the lecture.)

Listening for main ideas

___ More parents are involving their children in sports from a very young age.

___ Children's participation in sports is decreasing.

___ Learning to lose is an important lesson for life.

___ Research into children's sports is underfunded.

_1_ Participating in sports has many benefits for children.

___ Protecting children can actually lead to damaging children.

___ Sports-focused parents are often motivated by the prospect of financial gain.

___ The issue of cheating is growing in school sports.

___ When sports are part of a child's identity, there is a risk of negative effects.

Using Cornell notes for lectures

D Close listening

Having a system for note-taking helps to make your notes more effective. The Cornell system includes note-taking, asking questions, summarizing, reflecting, reviewing, and recalling.

Stage 1 Take notes

Write your notes in the note-taking column during the lecture. Use short, clear sentences.

Stage 2 Write questions

After the lecture, review your notes and write questions in the first column (e.g., *Is there any research on this? What could parents do differently?*). This will help you to identify connections and meaning. It will also help with later review work.

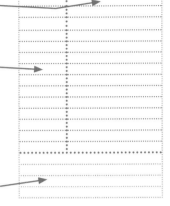

Stage 3 Summarize

Review your notes and questions and write a summary in the final section.

Stage 4 Reflect

Think about the content of the notes. How does it connect with other content? What is the background? Where does it take you next? Add ideas and questions to the first column.

Stage 5 Review and recall

Regularly spend a short time reviewing your notes. After reviewing, cover the second column and answer the questions in the first column.

1 🎧 **2.7** Imagine you are a sports-science student, listening to a sports psychology lecture. Listen to the first half of the lecture again and take notes in the second column. Compare your notes with a partner.

2 🎧 **2.8** Listen to the rest of the lecture and complete your notes in the second column. Again, compare your notes with a partner.

3 Review your notes and add questions to the first column. Then write a summary of the lecture. Compare your questions and summary with a partner. Revise as necessary.

E Critical thinking

Work in pairs. What other issues do children face in relation to sports? Brainstorm a list. Which has the greatest negative impact?

Critical thinking

Ad hominem attacks

When an argument is presented, we should consider counter arguments and criticism of the original viewpoint. However, this criticism should remain focused on the argument, and should not become personal.

An ad hominem attack is when the person making the argument is criticized rather than the argument itself. This is not a valid form of argument.

Avoid ad hominem attacks by staying focused on the ideas and argument, rather than thinking about the person who presented them.

1 Read the extracts from the discussion. Identify the ad hominem attacks. Which extract does not contain an ad hominem attack?

   1 A: It doesn't matter who is pleased by it ... we should just be trying to do the right thing.

        B: You always look for issues to be black and white, but they aren't.

   2 A: That was a very powerful point made in the third article, I thought anyhow.

        B: You would, though, wouldn't you ... I remember you telling me that you were a big fan of some of those cyclists who were implicated ...

   3 A: Sorry, sorry ... I was just saying ...

        B: OK, let's get back to the point ... Hana is right, I would say. There was no good argument against doping in any of the articles.

   4 A: And why not just have separate events for dopers and clean athletes, as is suggested?

        B: Hold on a minute ... you always do this ... make radical statements without thinking them through. How would we know they are clean?

2 Work with a partner. Rephrase the responses containing ad hominem attacks so they are focused on the argument rather than the person.

3 Why are ad hominem attacks not a valid form of argument? Discuss your ideas with a partner.

GAMES UNIT 2 35

Vocabulary development

Words for getting the opportunity to speak

1 Complete the expressions with a word from the box.

| back to | come | excuse | first | hold | same | straight | take |

1 Can I _____ in here?

2 I _____ your point.

3 Let's get something _____.

4 _____ me, but …

5 Let's get _____ the point.

6 _____ on a minute.

7 _____ and foremost …

8 All the _____ …

2 Match the expressions in Exercise 1 with the uses.

1 _____ to emphasize the main point

2 _____ to say something is true despite what was said before

3 _____ to show understanding of the previous point

4 _____ to show you don't think everyone understands

5 _____ to show you think a point needs correcting

6 _____ to show you think the discussion is irrelevant

7 _____ to pause the discussion

8 _____ to warn of an interruption

3 Work in groups of three. Students A and B discuss one of the issues below. Student C finds opportunities to speak using the phrases from Exercise 1. Change roles, and then change roles again.

- Parents are the most important sporting role models for their children.
- Schools shouldn't have sports teams until the students reach the age of 14.
- Some children are not naturally suited to sports, and we should accept that.

Academic words

1   Match the words in bold with the correct definitions.

1   **confined** (adj)
2   **exclude** (v)
3   **implicate** (v)
4   **inclination** (n)
5   **incompatible** (adj)
6   **inevitably** (adv)
7   **integration** (n)
8   **scenario** (n)

a   to make something seem likely to be the cause of something bad
b   limited to one area or group of people
c   a feeling that you want to do something
d   used for saying that something is certain to happen
e   not able to work or exist together because of basic differences
f   to deliberately not include something
g   a situation that could possibly happen
h   the process of combining with other things in a single larger group

2   Complete each sentence with your own ideas. Then compare your sentences with a partner. Which sentences do you most agree with, yours or your partner's?

1   Problems in sports are not **confined** to …
2   … often feel **excluded** from participating in sports.
3   If a sports competitor is **implicated** in doping, …
4   If a sports competitor has cheated once, the **inclination** of most people is …
5   Competitive sports are **incompatible** with …
6   Participating in contact sports **inevitably** leads to …
7   Local sports is … for **integration** in society.
8   Sports competitors have to consider a **scenario** in which they …

Speaking model

You are going to learn about expressing causality when you speak, using intonation to express and elicit information, and dealing with issues in group work. You are then going to take part in a discussion about sports.

A Analyze

Read the discussion. Answer the questions.

1 What problems are discussed?
2 What issues and interactions does the group experience in the discussion?

DANNI: So, remember, we are trying to establish which of the three problems is the biggest in the world of sports today. We also …

POPPY: Dangerous sports—you know, contact sports like rugby and boxing. That's what I think. I saw a really interesting program about them the other day …

DANNI: Maybe tell us about that later, Poppy.

POPPY: I don't mind telling you about it now. It was …

DANNI: Thanks, but we need to stay on track here. We need to discuss the different issues first before deciding. As I said, there are three we need to focus on—dangerous sports, of course. But then there's also sponsorship and the question of rivalry—by that I mean having too much competition between teams and even countries. Sal, do you want to tell us what you think?

SAL: Yes, sure. I think sponsorship is the most important one. For example, fast-food sponsorship can have a real effect on viewers, particularly younger people. They make that association between the unhealthy food and fit, active sports people. You all saw that last big competition?

DANNI: Yes, I did.

SAL: One of the major sponsors was a fast-food company.

DANNI: Yes, I know. Top sports players just don't eat or drink that stuff. But we see all this advertising at the sports events. As a result, we think they do … or at least, children think that. I agree—it's a big issue. Vera, what do you think? Which is the most significant in your opinion?

VERA: Uh, rivalry.

DANNI: Rivalry, that's interesting. Why do you say that?

VERA: Well, for example, in my country, we have a lot of problems with fighting at soccer games because there is so much rivalry between fans.

DANNI: And the police get involved?

VERA: Yes, and it costs a lot, in both time and money, to deal with.

SAL: Yes, that is a problem. And another consequence of this violence is that the general public stops going to these events. But I still think the long-term potential effect of sponsorship is more important. It affects millions of viewers, not just those at the event.

POPPY: But you would say that, wouldn't you? Because you don't eat fast food yourself, you think no one should.

SAL: No, it's not about my personal view. I've read the evidence.

B Discuss

Discuss the questions in a group. Explain and support your views.

1 Should dangerous sports be banned for adults and children?
2 Does it matter where sponsorship money comes from in sports?

Grammar

Expressing causality

We can show a cause-and-effect relationship in many ways. The grammar of the sentence depends on the particular words and phrases used to express the causality.

Because, so, as, since—before a clause

*They banned his new design of bikes **because** they were faster.*

Consequently, as a result—at the start of a sentence or after a semicolon

*… is very valuable. **As a result,** trying to eliminate loss actually destroys the main benefit of sports.*

Result from, lead to, have an effect on—main verbs followed by prepositions

*A lot of the health problems athletes suffer **result from** incorrect administration of drugs.*

A cause of, the impact of … on, a consequence of—noun phrases

*The problem is that **the impact of** the technology is not restricted to current swimmers.*

1   Complete the sentences with the correct word or phrase in the parentheses.

   1   **(As a result / Since / A cause of)**

   Top sports players don't eat or drink it, but we see all this advertising at the sports events. _____, we think they do.

   2   **(the impact of / consequently / an effect on)**

   For example, fast-food sponsorship can have _____ viewers, particularly younger people.

   3   **(because / lead to / a cause of)**

   In my country, we have a lot of problems with fighting at soccer games _____ there is so much rivalry between fans.

   4   **(as / consequence of / result from)**

   Another _____ this violence is that the general public stops going to these events.

2   Find the examples of cause-and-effect relationships in the model and check your answers.

3   Rephrase the sentences from Exercise 1 using a word or phrase of a different type to express causality.

Speaking skill

Group work is not always easy, and certain issues sometimes arise. For successful group work, the group needs to identify these issues and deal with them.

Unequal participation—everyone should contribute equally to the discussion.

Interruptions—group members need to be able to make their point before someone else speaks.

Unclear communication—expressing yourself clearly and listening carefully are important skills.

Going off topic—time is usually limited and the group needs to focus on the main points.

Ad hominem attacks—group discussion should focus on the topic, not criticism of individuals.

1 🎧 2.9 Listen to the extracts from the model and decide what the issue is that the speakers deal with.

	Issue	Phrase
1	_____	_____
2	_____	_____
3	_____	_____
4	_____	_____
5	_____	_____

2 🎧 2.9 Listen again and write the phrases used to deal with the issues.

3 Check your answers with the model. Then work with a partner to practice these parts of the model. One of you creates the issue, and the other responds with the phrase.

4 Work in groups of five. Each person should adopt an issue from the skills box. Discuss the following statement. Work as a group to deal with each issue as it arises.

   Governments should spend more money on free sports facilities for the public.

5 Change issues and discuss the same statement. Does the group deal with the issues better this time?

Pronunciation for speaking

Intonation when expressing and eliciting information

Intonation helps us to communicate more clearly. The pitch of our voice going up or down can show if we are giving information or asking for it. The grammar usually supports this, but intonation on its own can show this. The biggest pitch change happens on the most stressed word in the statement or question.

Do you play **team** *sports?*   *You play* **team** *sports?*   *You play* **team** *sports.*

However, information questions (with question words such as *what, who,* etc.), can have a similar intonation pattern to statements. The question word tells the listener that information is being elicited.

What **team** *sports do you play?*

1   🎧 2.10 Listen to the short extracts from the Speaking model. Decide if the person is expressing or eliciting information.

   1   expressing / eliciting   _____
   2   expressing / eliciting   _____
   3   expressing / eliciting   _____
   4   expressing / eliciting   _____
   5   expressing / eliciting   _____
   6   expressing / eliciting   _____
   7   expressing / eliciting   _____

2   Review the Speaking model.

   1   Find the extracts in the Speaking model and practice giving and asking for information.

   2   Find an example of an information question. Practice it.

3   Write two questions about sports to match the intonation patterns above. Then ask your partner the questions.

   A   _____
       _____
   B   _____
       _____

Speaking task

Have a group discussion to evaluate problems in the world of sports.

Brainstorm

Review *Technology in sports* and *Children, sports, and identity* and the Speaking section.

- Make a list of the main problems discussed, e.g., doping in sports. Add one more of your own.
- Add notes that may be useful when you discuss these problems, e.g., evidence and arguments.
- Write two questions for each of the problems to explore them further, e.g., *How much money is spent investigating doping in sports?*
- Research facts and statistics to answer your questions.

Plan

Review and organize your notes. Make a preliminary evaluation of the problems, identifying the most and least important.

Speak

Work in a group. Evaluate problems in the world of sports. Your group's goal is to agree on the most significant and the least significant problem in sports.

Deal with issues that arise in the group to stay on task.

Share

Work with a new group. Share your experiences of the discussion. Did you reach your goal? How well did your group deal with issues that arose?

Reflect

Using your learning from this unit, answer the questions.

1 What are some common issues in group work?
2 What factors should be considered when evaluating problems?
3 What is more important in sports, the outcome or the participation?

Review

Wordlist

MACMILLAN DICTIONARY

Vocabulary preview

eliminate (v) **	irrelevant (adj) **	restricted (adj) *
elite (n) **	motivate (v) **	risk (n) ***
enhance (v) **	outrage (n) *	ultimate (adj) **
fundamental (adj) ***	prestige (n)	unscrupulous (adj)
initiative (n) ***	prolonged (adj)	
interfere (v) **	protective (adj) **	

Vocabulary development

come in here	get back to the point	take your point
first and foremost	get something straight	

Academic words

confined (adj)	incompatible (adj)
exclude (v) ***	inevitably (adv) **
implicate (v)	integration (n) **
inclination (n)*	scenario (n) *

Academic words review

Complete the sentences with the correct form of the words in the box.

| confined | exclude | implicate | integration | scenario |

1 Once the children learned everyone's names, the _____ was easy.
2 We decided to _____ the managers from this meeting to give everyone a chance to speak freely.
3 Studies seemed to _____ sportspeople and their coaches in several scandals last year.
4 The _____ for these interviews is simple: one person asks all the questions.
5 Deborah did not react well to being locked in a _____ space.

Unit review

Listening 1	☐	I can follow the way a discussion develops.
Listening 2	☐	I can use Cornell notes for lectures.
Study skill	☐	I can use techniques for speaking up in a discussion.
Vocabulary	☐	I can use phrases for getting the opportunity to speak.
Grammar	☐	I can express causality.
Speaking	☐	I can speak up to take part in a discussion.

Discussion point

Study the infographic about the way people respond to change, and answer the questions.

1 What factors influence which path we take in the change process?

2 How can we help ourselves or others to manage change?

3 Which stage requires the most energy to complete? Why?

4 What should "change managers" or "change coaches" do at the start of and during the process?

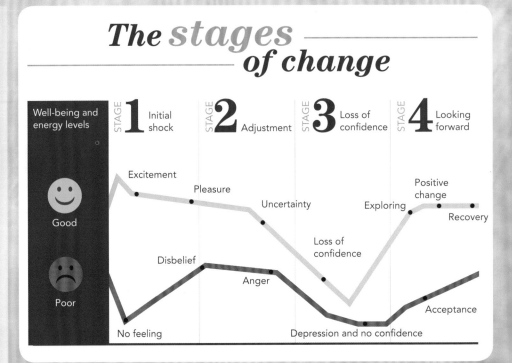

The stages of change

VIDEO

OLD BUILDINGS, NEW ENERGY

Before you watch

Match the words in bold with the correct definitions.

1	**algorithm** (n)	a	a limitation or restriction
2	**binder** (n)	b	a roof in the form of an arch
3	**constraint** (n)	c	a set of computer calculations
4	**heritage** (n)	d	a substance used to make things stick together
5	**mortar** (n)	e	a substance used to stick bricks together
6	**vault** (n)	f	historical features belonging to a culture

UNIT AIMS

LISTENING 1 Recognizing allusions to external events
LISTENING 2 Listening to annotate presentation slides
STUDY SKILL Group presentations

VOCABULARY Words for change situations
GRAMMAR Conditional language
SPEAKING Referring to other speakers

Recovering energy during a short nap.

While you watch

Watch the video and choose *T* (True) or *F* (False).

1. Scientists are using a computer algorithm to discover new ways of building. T / F
2. The gothic architects of the past used complex machinery to construct their buildings. T / F
3. Using gothic geometry, researchers have been able to build structures using sand. T / F
4. The structures are more than 50% lighter than those made with concrete. T / F
5. Only sand can be used with this building technique. T / F

After you watch

Discuss these questions in a group.

1. Why do you think the traditional building techniques were forgotten?
2. Why do you think buildings in the past were so much more beautiful than modern buildings?
3. What are the most impressive historical buildings you have seen?
4. Which do you prefer to live in, modern or more traditional buildings? Why?
5. What other ways do you think computers are helping us to understand our past?

Managing change

A Vocabulary preview

1   Match the words in bold with the correct definitions.

1	**capability** (n)	a	not obvious and therefore difficult to notice
2	**complexity** (n)	b	a rule or situation that puts a limit on something
3	**limitation** (n)	c	a particular way of doing something
4	**mode** (n)	d	not willing to do something
5	**pursue** (v)	e	the ability to do something
6	**reluctant** (adj)	f	the complicated nature of something
7	**subtle** (adj)	g	the process of changing from one state to another
8	**transition** (n)	h	to follow a course of activity

2   Complete the sentences with the words from the boxes. Change the form if necessary.

capability   limitations   reluctant   subtle

1   When we are under pressure to change, we very quickly find out our

_____.

2   Many organizations do not have the _____ to change fast enough for today's world.

3   Some people are naturally _____ to accept change; they were born that way.

4   Managers need to be _____ when managing change: they should avoid ordering people to change.

complexity   mode   pursue   transition

5   Any _____ period is always stressful for those people involved.

6   Not many people have the skills to handle the _____ of making major changes in a company.

7   Employees should be free to _____ their own goals rather than work toward the company goals.

8   Survival _____ will get you through the period of change, but you need to take some action as well.

B Before you listen

Work in a group. What kind of major changes can take place in these places?

cities   companies   educational institutions   governments

C Global listening

1   🎧 **3.1** You will hear part of a discussion about change. Answer the questions.

   1   Where is the change happening?

   2   What is happening as part of the change?

2   🎧 **3.2** Listen to the whole discussion. Choose the best word to complete the sentences.

Listening to the way a discussion develops

   1   Max **explains / questions** the reason he is there.

   2   Alex describes the **uncertainty / confidence** he and others are feeling.

   3   Eileen shows **excitement / disbelief**.

   4   John is **happy / concerned** about the energy spent doing past work.

   5   Max **encourages /orders** the group to think positively.

   6   John **argues that / questions whether** change is necessary.

   7   Max recommends that they **reject / accept** the changes.

   8   Max **explains / denies** that the process could be difficult.

   9   John expresses **insecurity / excitement** about work.

  10   Max advises that individuals **can / cannot** choose to experience change positively or not.

  11   Eileen **identifies / denies** the difficulty with any process of change.

  12   Max is pleased that Eileen **likes / understands** the change process.

D Close listening

Speakers sometimes make indirect references, or *allusions*. These can refer to external events or people, and the references are made without additional detail or information.

*I'm a change coach, and, **as the big boss might have told you**, I'm here to help with "the transition."*

Recognizing allusions helps you to understand the "bigger picture," that is, the context and history of the topic currently under discussion.

When making an allusion, the speaker may use emphasis and pauses. If you are watching the speaker, look for hand gestures and facial expressions.

*We have heard something about these **"secret talks,"** but no one …*

1 🎧 **3.2** Listen to the discussion again and choose the correct answers.

1 The phrase "that meeting" mentioned by Alex refers to **a positive, good meeting / a small, unimportant meeting / a difficult meeting people still talk about**.

2 When Alex says "they've decided we're going to…," she views both parties as **very unequal / open and communicative / without any problems**.

3 Eileen thinks people were going to be asked about their opinions because **her colleague told her so / someone important said this at a meeting / it is the right thing to happen**.

4 Jill in HR is **quite well-known to everybody at this meeting / new to the company / arguing against all change**.

5 Max assumes that this year's conference **wasn't well attended / didn't have much to do with change / had a memorable and relevant topic**.

6 Max tries to defend **the people who employed him / the staff who have to go through the change / himself and his job title**.

7 Max is confident that the staff **is aware they will get training / will be happy with all the changes / will have no problem with the process**.

8 Max and Eileen **definitely never met / met a few weeks ago / probably exchanged emails**.

2 🎧 **3.3** Review the skills box. Then listen again to the allusions and make a note of phrases and pronunciation indicating they are allusions.

E Critical thinking

What kind of changes have places where you live, study, or work faced? Identify a major change and discuss with a partner who managed the change and how people were affected.

Study skills   Group presentations

Presenters aim to communicate information and ideas clearly: Their audience is the main focus of the presentation. This is the same for groups and individuals. For a successful presentation:

- *Focus on a few main points and select concrete examples that are easy to visualize.*
- *Structure the talk clearly, make links between your points, and summarize at the end.*
- *Use a visual display or handout to show the presentation plan to the audience.*

In group presentations, the presenters work together, contributing equally, to deliver their presentation to their audience. Further tasks as group presenters are to:

- *Assign roles to each presenter.*
- *Decide who will present each point.*
- *Identify how to support the person speaking.*
- *Agree on a strategy for dealing with questions.*

© Stella Cottrell (2013)

1 Work in a group. Discuss the following question in relation to the seven points in the Study skills box.

What might happen if you do not do this?

Example

If we focus on more than a few main points, then the presentation will be confusing and …

2 Work in the same group. Choose a topic to present from the list. Follow the steps for a successful group presentation as you prepare.

Recognizing allusions to external events

Stages within change management

How to give an effective group presentation

3 Watch another group's presentation. Make notes and give feedback on the following:

Clarity _____

Organization _____

Group collaboration _____

Perspectives on the past

A Vocabulary preview

1 Match the words in the box with the correct definitions.

> instinct legacy phenomena predecessor
> prone reminder strategic trigger

1 _____ carefully planned in order to achieve a particular goal
2 _____ a natural tendency to behave in a particular way
3 _____ events or situations that can be seen to happen or exist
4 _____ likely to be affected by something, especially something bad
5 _____ something such as a tradition that exists as a result of the past
6 _____ something or someone that has been replaced by another thing or person
7 _____ something that reminds you of something that happened in the past
8 _____ to make something happen

2 Complete the sentences using your own ideas.

1 I would ask my **predecessors** in any situation …
2 When the group I am in faces problems, my **instinct** is to …
3 It is … to surround yourself with **reminders** of a time in the past that is over.
4 … always **triggers** happy memories for me.
5 I … the **phenomenon** of feeling sad but happy about the past.
6 I am **prone** to feelings of … when I think about …
7 I … make **strategic** plans for …
8 … should consider the **legacy** they will leave.

3 Compare your sentences from Exercise 2 with a partner. How many of each other's ideas do you agree with?

B Before you listen

You are going to listen to a group presentation about the past. First, discuss the scenarios below with a partner.

Scenarios	Order in presentation	Referred to as …
1 You are in a line. You have waited for one hour already, and you don't feel you are any closer to the front. **What do you do?**	___	___
2 Your computer, which contains all your photos, music, favorite URLs, etc., is set up with the printer and other computers in the house and you use it all day, every day. However, it is very slow. **Do you get a new one?**	___	___
3 You arrive at a family member's house and smell the same type of cake baking that you ate as a child. You haven't eaten it for years. **How do you feel?**	___	___

C Global listening

1 🎧 **3.4** Listen to the introduction to the presentation and complete the table in the previous exercise.

Listening for organization and key terms

> legacy   negative energy   nostalgia   sunk-cost fallacy

1 In which order will the scenarios be mentioned in the presentation? Number the scenarios (1–3).

2 What is the name used for the concepts described in each scenario? Complete the table with the terms in the box. One term is extra.

2 🎧 **3.5** Listen to the rest of the lecture and number the ideas (1–10) in the order they are presented.

	Order
We need to examine our natural desire to continue.	___
This is a natural, though often wrong, thing to do.	___
Many in the business world advise giving up on the situation.	_5_
Very large systems can be very difficult to change.	___
We feel we tried hard in the past and shouldn't waste this effort.	___
People often don't want to change or don't see the need.	___
Music, smells, old friends, and bad moods often lead to this feeling.	___
If companies don't change, they may become less competitive.	___
This feeling creates changes in the brain.	_1_
The most important thing to focus on is the end result.	___

Listening to annotate
presentation slides

D Close listening

Presenters often provide handouts of their presentation slides. Annotate the handout to provide a complete record of the presentation.

- *Check that slide details include the speaker's name, and the title, location, and date of the presentation.*
- *Identify the structure of the talk by indicating slides that give the overview or main points.*
- *Add additional examples and points given by the lecturer.*
- *Note the speaker's conclusions in more detail.*
- *Include a note of any references made to other sources or speakers.*

Build on the information provided in the handout in the following ways:

- *Make connections between the ideas on different slides with arrows.*
- *Write your own questions and ideas on the relevant slides.*
- *Indicate areas you need more clarity on.*

1 🎧 **3.4** Listen to the first part of the presentation. Annotate slides 1–3 below.

2 🎧 **3.5** Listen to the presentation. Annotate slides 4–9 on page 188.

1 Perspectives on the past	2 Nostalgia	3 Nostalgia
Nostalgia Professor Simpson **Sunk-cost fallacy** Dr. Hossam **Legacy systems** Stephen Johnson	**Universal experience** • From an early age • All cultures	**Brain changes** Specific brain pattern **Triggers** e.g., music, bad moods

E Critical thinking

Which of the three ideas is most harmful? What makes you think that?

Critical thinking

Making deductions

We make deductions when we use the available evidence to come to a logical conclusion. A logical conclusion is more than just a summary of fact and/or argument. It includes a judgment based on a line of reasoning.

Change can be difficult.
Many people prefer an easy life.
Therefore, many people are not comfortable with change.

Listen for phrases that indicate such a judgment has been made:

This leads us to ...
This means that...
Consequently,

Useful deductions need a clear line of reasoning and firm evidence (which can be supported).

Problems can occur when conclusions include evidence that is not contained in the line of reasoning, or when the line of reasoning is not clear.

Organizational change needs everyone to join in.
Everyone joining in makes things easier.
This means that organizational change is easy.

1   Are the conclusions in these deductions logical?

   1   Music and food from our youth are strong triggers of nostalgia. Many older people enjoy experiencing nostalgia. Consequently, many older people still enjoy music and food from their youth.

   2   Students like using technology. We can use technology for learning. This leads us to believe students like learning.

   3   Change coaches have experience in managing change. Managing change is difficult for inexperienced people. This means that we should hire a change coach to manage the change in our organization.

2   What evidence might these conclusions be based on? Discuss in a group.

   1   Younger people like change more than older people do.

   2   Change can energize people and improve their performance.

   3   Organizational change costs a lot of money.

3   In your experience, are the conclusions from Exercise 1 logical? Discuss your views and summarize the main points for the class.

Vocabulary development

Words for change situations

1 Match the words in the box with the correct meanings.

| initiate | outcome | persist | prevailing |
| resilient | sacrifice | tendency | variable |

1 _____ (n) a strong chance that something will happen in a particular way

2 _____ (adj) able to quickly become healthy, happy, or strong again after a problem

3 _____ (adj) existing at a particular time or in a particular place

4 _____ (n) something that can change and affect the result of a situation

5 _____ (n) the final result of a process

6 _____ (v) to continue to do or say something in a determined way

7 _____ (v) to give up something important so that you or others can have something else

8 _____ (v) to make something start

2 Complete the sentences with your own ideas.

1 The best way to **initiate** major change in a company is to …

2 Many people's energy levels have a **tendency** to … when change is involved.

3 In difficult times, it is better to focus on the **outcome** rather than …

4 Many people will make a **sacrifice** as long as …

5 The **prevailing** view of change and development is …

6 Being **resilient** is a useful quality when …

7 Some of the **variables** in any change process are …

8 It is important to find energy and **persist** when …

3 Compare and discuss your sentences with a partner. How many do you agree on?

Academic words

1 Match the words in bold with the correct definitions.

1	**adaptation** (n)	a	changing into something completely different, or the process by which this happens
2	**assurance** (n)		
3	**criteria** (n)	b	a feeling or attitude of confidence
4	**mechanism** (n)	c	a particular area of interest, activity, work, etc., that is one of many parts of life
5	**norm** (n)		
6	**sphere** (n)	d	a situation in which things happen as they should and there are no harmful changes
7	**stability** (n)		
8	**transformation** (n)	e	a system of parts that people think of as working together like parts of a machine
		f	something that is usual or expected
		g	standards that are used for judging something or for making a decision about something
		h	the process of changing something so that it can be used for a different purpose

2 Complete each sentence with a word in bold from Exercise 1.

1 Most people prefer _____ to change, even if there are problems with the present system.

2 Going through the process of _____ to any new situation can be personally challenging.

3 At work, it is important to agree on _____ that will determine what is typical.

4 _____ of any type, personal or professional, is always difficult and can become costly.

5 Nostalgia is a/an _____ that reminds us of the good times in our past.

6 Managers should use their _____ of influence to spread positive messages about change.

7 Companies must give a/an _____ that services will be improved by changes to the system.

8 There are no _____ to help us decide if we should forget about past investments and move on.

3 Choose the three sentences you most disagree with from Exercise 2. Explain your choices to a partner. Does your partner share your view?

Speaking model

You are going to learn about using conditional language when you speak, preparing and rehearsing talking points, and referring to other speakers. You are then going to participate in a group presentation proposing solutions for dealing with change.

A Analyze

Read the discussion. Answer the questions.

1 What might be the issue they are talking about? Why do you think that?

2 Which people are mentioned as being involved in the issue?

3 What is one problem identified?

HANA: The three of us presenting our solutions today all come from different backgrounds in relation to the problem. This ought to provide a broader perspective on the issue and some more innovative solutions. First, I'm going to outline the basic issue, along with the main problems I identified. Then Ella will talk about one of the problems from a student's perspective. In the last part, Julia will bring in the teachers' point of view. We will take questions at the end, providing there is time. If not, we can meet informally in the school cafeteria to continue the discussion there.

...

ELLA: Coming back to Hana's point about the cost of making these changes, we need to think about how much of this will be passed on to students. Supposing fees were dramatically increased? How many students would still apply to come here? The priority for many students is affordable fees. Raise the prices, and they may seek cheaper courses elsewhere, or online. Julia will talk more about how the cost of the changes may affect teachers, but I think we can guess they won't be happy with a pay freeze.

...

JULIA: The problems can be solved. As both Hana and Ella have said, change is difficult, and people don't like it at first. However, as long as it's managed effectively, everyone can benefit in the final outcome—the management, the teachers, and current and future students. People need to be able to feel valued in the process. And feeling valued comes from being listened to. Therefore, it's vital that the management set up feedback groups for both teachers and students.

...

HANA: Does anyone have a question?

AUDIENCE MEMBER: Yes, I do. What do you think the majority of students think about this?

HANA: I'll hand this question over to Ella. She's focusing on the student perspective. Ella?

ELLA: Thanks, Hana, yes, ...

B Discuss

1 Identify three reasons and three conclusions in the model.

2 What do you think of the conclusions? Discuss your views in a group.

Grammar

Conditional language

We use conditional language to discuss unreal situations; these situations could be probable, possible, unlikely, or even impossible. We use conditional language when we imagine these situations and we want to discuss their possible outcomes or consequences.
If the company hired a change coach, they would be able to manage the process better.

The conditional clause most often uses *if*, but it can also use other markers.

To mean *if … not*: **unless**
Unless the employees change their attitude, the process will be very difficult.

For both real and imaginary conditions:
provided that / providing   as long as / so long as
Nostalgia can be a positive experience, providing it doesn't dominate your life.

For imaginary conditions: **supposing / suppose that   assuming**
Supposing your company decides to change the system, how will you cope?

For outcomes that are likely if the condition is not fulfilled: **otherwise**
The company needs to change its system. Otherwise, their competitors will take their customers.

1 🎧 **3.6** Find the conditional marker, and then match the parts of the conditional sentences. Listen and check.

1 Provided that you learn the new skills required,   it won't be like that.

   The French writer Proust springs to mind,   assuming you are familiar with his novels.

2 Unless we adapt immediately,   otherwise that might happen.

   You'll need to learn some new skills required,   we're in danger of losing our jobs.

2 Identify the conditional marker. Then complete these sentences with your ideas.

1 Unless big companies change their IT systems, …
2 As long as a company manages change sensitively, …
3 Supposing my school wants to make big changes, …
4 … . Otherwise, the company is sure to fail.
5 … , providing enough training and support is given by the management.
6 … , assuming everyone is enthusiastic and ready for the change.

3 Compare your sentences with a partner. First, check that the grammar is correct. Then give your opinion on the statement.

Speaking skill

When we present ideas as a group, we can use our knowledge of what the other speakers are going to say or have said. Referring forward and backward helps to make links clear for the audience.

X will explain more about …   This will be picked up by …
As X has already said …   As already highlighted by X …
Picking up on what X said …
As X said earlier,   … what our previous speakers were describing.
Coming back to X's point …

As well as using references to make connections for the audience, presenters can refer to other speakers for support.

Perhaps X would like to come in here.
This isn't really my area. X, you've looked into this more.
I'll hand this question over to X, who …

1 🎧 **3.7** Listen and make a note of the phrases used to refer to other speakers. Check your answers with the phrases from the skills box.

1 The practical aspects of this _____ by Dr. Hossam _F_

2 And then we can use this understanding in the field of behavioral sciences, which Dr. Hossam _____ ___

3 On the surface, it may not seem to have much to do with _____ ___

4 This sunk-cost fallacy does seem to be an inherited instinct, similar to nostalgia, _____ Professor Simpson ___

5 Now, the connection to Professor Simpson's area should be becoming evident … _____, nostalgia is a neurological phenomenon ___

6 And _____ Dr. Hossam, the sunk-cost fallacy is a factor in any decision ___

2 Review the sentences from Exercise 1. Identify the sentences that refer to *B* (Back) and those that refer to *F* (Forward).

3 Review the model and underline the phrases used to refer to other speakers for support. What reasons might a speaker have for doing this?

4 Work in groups and choose one topic together for a mini-presentation.

    finding energy to face changes   nostalgia   schools and technology

5 Practice your mini-presentation. Use phrases from the skills box to:

    • refer to what other speakers will or have said.

    • get support.

Pronunciation for speaking

Preparing and rehearsing talking points

Effective pronunciation ensures your audience can engage with your ideas. Focus on the key features to makes your delivery successful:

1 Make sure you are very confident with the pronunciation of key terms and names. Correct word stress is important for the audience to understand multi-syllable words.

2 Use sentence stress to highlight the key points, emphasizing the main syllables in these words.

3 Insert short pauses between groups of words and longer pauses between sentences.

4 Indicate when a point is finished by using falling intonation.

Use these strategies:

• Mark these four pronunciation features on your presentation script.

• Practice several times.

• Record yourself and analyze your performance.

*The **three** of us ⬆ ¦ presenting our solutions today ⬆ ¦ **all come** ⬆ ¦ from different **back**grounds ⬆ ¦ in relation ⬆ ¦ to the **problem**. ⬇ ¦¦ This ought to pro**vide** ⬆ ¦ a **broad**er perspective ⬆ ¦ on the **issue** ⬆ ¦ and some **more innovative** solutions. ⬇ ¦¦*

1 🎧 **3.8** Listen and mark the sentence stress, pauses, and intonation on the extracts from the Speaking model.

  1 Coming back to Hana's point about the cost of making these changes, we need to think about how much this will be passed on to students.

  2 The problems can be solved. As both Hana and Ella have said, change is difficult, and people don't like it at first.

2 🎧 **3.9** Mark the pronunciation features on the extracts from the Speaking model. Then listen and check.

  1 First, I'm going to outline the basic issue, along with the main problems I identified.

  2 Supposing fees were dramatically increased? How many students would still apply to come here?

  3 However, as long as it is managed effectively, everyone can benefit in the final outcome—the management, the teachers, and current and future students.

3 Work with a partner. Deliver the parts of the presentation in Exercises 1 and 2, using the marked pronunciation features to help.

Speaking task

Give a group presentation about proposed solutions for dealing with change.

Brainstorm

Review *Managing change* and *Perspectives on the past* and the Speaking lesson, identifying problems associated with change and strategies to manage these problems.

Case study: *A school has decided all teachers need to deliver at least 50% of their courses online. Right now, courses are delivered 100% face to face.*

Read the case study and identify the key issues and the people involved in the situation. Speculate on problems that may occur. Make preliminary notes on possible solutions.

Work in a group. Discuss the key issues in the case study and share your ideas on possible solutions. One member of the group should take notes.

Plan

Together, review your notes. Reach an agreement on the number of main points to present and possible solutions to propose. Assign roles and decide who will make each point. Consider your audience, prepare your presentation, and practice giving it effectively.

Speak

Give your presentation, identifying problems and proposing solutions. Deal with questions at the end of the presentation.

Share

Work with a new group. Discuss the process of preparing and giving your group presentation. What were the challenges? What strategies helped?

Reflect

Using the information you learned throughout the unit, answer the questions.

1 What are the challenges and benefits of giving a group presentation?
2 What can we gain from reflecting on the past?
3 Which is more challenging to deal with, change or continuity?

Review

Wordlist

MACMILLAN DICTIONARY

Vocabulary preview

capability (n) **	phenomena (n) **	strategic (adj) **
complexity (n) **	predecessor (n) **	subtle (adj) **
instinct (n) **	prone (adj) *	transition (n) **
legacy (n) **	pursue (v) **	trigger (v) **
limitation (n) **	reluctant (adj) **	
mode (n) **	reminder (n) **	

Vocabulary development

initiate (v) **	prevailing (adj) *	tendency (n) **
outcome (n) ***	resilient (adj)	variable (n) **
persist (v) **	sacrifice (v) *	

Academic words

adaptation (n) *	mechanism (n) **	stability (n) **
assurance (n) **	norm (n) **	transformation (n) **
criteria (n) ***	sphere (n) **	

Academic words review

Complete the sentences with the correct form of the words in the box.

adaptation	inclination	inevitably	norm	stability

1　Noor's test result was great—definitely an exception from the _____.
2　All sports fields closed last year. _____, students protested.
3　His novel was better than the film _____ that followed.
4　People are frustrated at the college dean's _____ to hold meetings at short notice.
5　It's good to see some _____ in this team after so many changes.

Unit review

Listening 1	☐	I can recognize allusions to external events.
Listening 2	☐	I can listen to annotate presentation slides.
Study skill	☐	I can improve and contribute to group presentations.
Vocabulary	☐	I can use words describing change situations.
Grammar	☐	I can use conditional language.
Speaking	☐	I can refer to other speakers when discussing things.

Discussion point

Study the infographic about stages in group work, and answer the questions.

1 What are the key functions and feelings of each stage of group work?

2 In your experience, do groups usually follow these stages?

3 What might the risks be at each stage? Which stage has the most risks?

4 Is group work always the most appropriate method of working?

The life of A GROUP

 Stage 1:
Forming

actions:
> establish roles and rules
> set goals

members:
> positive
> polite
> nervous

 Stage 2:
Storming

actions:
> competition for leadership
> question goals

members:
> competitive
> challenged
> uncomfortable

 **Stage 3:**
Norming

actions:
> respond to feedback
> work toward goals

members:
> respect
> understanding
> interdependence

 Stage 4:
Performing

actions:
> achieve goals
> plan for the future

members:
> self-managing
> fulfilled
> positive

© 2014 Zen Ex Machina Pty Ltd.

VIDEO

POWERCHAIR SOCCER

Before you watch

Match the words in bold with the correct definitions.

1 **association** (n)   a a group of people with a shared purpose

2 **assumption** (n)   b something that is believed without proof

3 **bid** (v)   c to kill or injure someone with a car

4 **gear up** (v)   d to move at speed

5 **run over** (v)   e to prepare

6 **whip around** (v)   f to try to do something

UNIT AIMS

LISTENING 1 Identifying consensus in group speech
LISTENING 2 Listening for speculation and degree of certainty
STUDY SKILL Studying collaboratively

VOCABULARY Words for risk and conflict
GRAMMAR Hedging
SPEAKING Obtaining consensus

A risky ascent.

While you watch

Watch the video and choose *T* (True) or *F* (False).

1 It can be dangerous.   T / F
2 It is played on a soccer field.   T / F
3 They use the same type of ball as in soccer.   T / F
4 There are the same number of players as in
   a soccer team.   T / F
5 The game is exciting to play.   T / F

After you watch

Discuss these questions in a group.

1 Would you like to play powerchair soccer?
   Why / why not?
2 Have you ever watched the Paralympic Games?
3 Which sports do you like to play and watch?
4 What's the most dangerous / exciting thing you
   have done?
5 Have you ever been to a sports stadium for an
   international event?

Rule breakers, risk-takers

A Vocabulary preview

1 Match the words in bold with the correct definitions.

1 **argumentative** (adj) a often disagreeing with people
2 **dysfunctional** (adj) b to follow a course of activity
3 **maverick** (adj and n) c a range of marks used to measure something
4 **proportion** (n) d an independent person with different ideas and behavior
5 **pursue** (v) e the relationship between two or more quantities
6 **risk-taker** (n) f a person who is not afraid, and often does things differently
7 **scale** (n) g different from what most people consider to be normal
8 **unconventional** (adj) h not working in a successful or even normal way

2 Complete the extract with the words in bold from Exercise 1.

¹ _____Mavericks_____ are increasingly being seen as important in the world of work. These ² _____, previously perceived negatively and often blamed for causing ³ _____ groups due to their ⁴ _____ style in discussion, are now being re-assessed. Their ⁵ _____ behavior in their desire to ⁶ _____ their goals is now recognized as a strength in the workplace. The task now for employers is to accurately assess their employees on the ⁷ _____ of maverick behavior and ensure they hire the correct ⁸ _____ of mavericks to team players.

B Before you listen

Preparing to listen

Work in a group. Discuss the questions.

1 What skills and qualities do companies typically value in people they hire?
2 What risks might there be for a company in hiring someone with maverick qualities?
3 What benefits might a maverick new hire bring?

C Global listening

1 🎧 **4.1** Listen to the start of a discussion about mavericks. Complete the agenda for the discussion.

> **Economics course E1035**
>
> **Discussion group C**
>
> **Discussion aim:** To make recommendations on the proportion of mavericks a company should hire
>
> **Points to discuss:**
>
> How many to _____
>
> How to _____
>
> How to _____

2 🎧 **4.2** Read the list of topics. Then listen to the next part of the discussion, and number the topics in the order they are discussed. (One of them is not discussed.)

___ How to help mavericks work with a team

___ Group work issues with mavericks

___ Balancing different types of people for success

___ The possible benefits of introducing a maverick into a group

___ Dealing with problems created by mavericks

___ A method for measuring maverick behavior

_1_ The opposing views of the term *maverick*

___ Issues with assessing maverick behavior

Identifying consensus in
group speech

D Close listening

> To understand the flow and outcomes of a discussion, it helps to identify
> when the participants:
>
> - *agree on a point*   *I think we all agree in principle that …*
>
> - *disagree on a point*   *I agree with you on the whole, but the
>   particular problem with that is …*
>   *Let's agree to disagree.*
>
> - *move on from the point*   *Let's move on …*
>   *We can return to this point later.*
>
> - *return to or "revisit" a point*   *Coming back to …*
>   *To return to our previous point …*
>
> Consensus is achieved when everyone agrees.

1 🎧 **4.3** Listen to parts of the discussion again. What do the speakers,
   individually or as a group, do in each extract? (It could be more than
   one thing.)

   Extract 1 _____   A   disagree on a point
   Extract 2 _____   B   suggest the discussion moves on
   Extract 3 _____   C   return to a point
   Extract 4 _____   D   achieve consensus

2 🎧 **4.3** Listen again and make a note of the words and phrases that helped
   you to decide.

E Critical thinking

1 Think of two people you know at either end of the maverick scale. Describe
   their behavior to your group. Evaluate how effective the behavior of each
   person is in their respective contexts.

   Strong group-focused behavior   Strong maverick behavior

2 Discuss the questions.

   1   How do we define success in a group task—process or outcome?
   2   Does it matter how we reach a successful outcome?

Study skills | Studying collaboratively

There are many skills to gain from studying collaboratively. Through working with others, you develop awareness and understanding of:

- group dynamics
- how others think and feel
- what motivates people
- how to use skills and time most effectively.

Collaborative work gives us the opportunity to help others to contribute and also to receive feedback on and improve our own performance. Developing these skills can be challenging, and we need to be prepared to take some risks. We need to:

- listen to others
- develop our own self-awareness
- at times, prioritize the interests of the group above our own.

© Stella Cottrell (2013)

1   In which situations have you or will you have to work collaboratively on your course? Make a list, and then compare your list with your group.

Example:

Tutorials

Work placement

2   Identify a successful group collaboration you have been part of. Consider the questions below and share your answers with your group.

1   What form did the collaboration take?

2   How did the collaboration affect the group members in terms of the following?

      goals   responsibility   roles   tasks

3   How did you benefit from being part of that group?

4   What did you learn from the experience that has helped you in collaborative work since then?

3   Add to the list of positive aspects of collaborative work.

Learning to be more assertive

Receiving support from others

Achieving more than you could on your own

Developing your understanding of other perspectives

Sharing …

Learning …

Developing …

Understanding …

Receiving …

Enjoying …

4   Discuss your lists in a group. Can you agree on the top five most valuable aspects of collaborative work?

Managing risk

A Vocabulary preview

1 Match the words in bold with the correct definitions.

1	**assign** (v)	a	something that gets your attention and prevents you from concentrating
2	**comprehensive** (adj)		
3	**confidential** (adj)	b	in a situation with no other people
4	**distraction** (n)	c	to make something less strong
5	**momentum** (n)	d	including many details or aspects of something
6	**preconception** (n)	e	an opinion of something formed before having a lot of information or experience of it
7	**solitary** (adj)		
8	**weaken** (v)	f	to give someone something to do
		g	progress or development that is becoming faster or stronger
		h	describing something that must be kept secret

2 Complete the sentences to give your opinion.

1 The biggest **distraction** from study for most people is …
2 Doing **comprehensive** research means you …
3 **Solitary** study spaces are …
4 **Assigning** roles in groups is …
5 Once the **momentum** in a group starts, it is …
6 Many students have **preconceptions** about …
7 **Confidential** information should …
8 Failing to deal with problems in a group can **weaken** …

3 Compare your sentences from Exercise 2 with a partner.

B Before you listen

1 Tell your partner about a group you are part of right now.

In the "Forming, Storming, Norming, Performing" model, which stage is the group at?

What indicates the group is at this stage?

2 What limitations might there be with this theory of group development?

C Global listening

1 ⊕ 4.4 Listen to the start of a lecture about conflict in groups. What limitations does the speaker identify with the "Forming, Storming, Norming, Performing" model of group development?

2 ⊕ 4.5 Read the sentence parts and predict how to match them. Then listen to the rest of the lecture to check.

Predicting

1 The first risk to the company was that the project

2 The second risk was that the company employees

3 Intragroup conflict happens when team members

4 Specific practical factors such as an unfair benefit system

5 Changing routines established in the early phases

6 Task conflict comes from lack of agreement on how to

7 Problems often arise when more than one manager

8 Limiting the time available

9 Having two isolated teams with different values

a works on a project.

b is not as effective as one team.

c fight with each other.

d can cause stress and conflict.

e might not succeed.

f complete a task.

g can help a team.

h can improve performance.

i might fail as a team.

Listening for speculation and degree of certainty

D Close listening

Academic speakers often consider possible outcomes, and indicate how certain they are about the issues discussed. To understand the perspective of an academic speaker more fully, listen for language used for:

Speculation   might   may   could
Degree of certainty   must   is obviously   almost certainly   possibly

Also, listen for the amount of emphasis the speaker places on different points through the use of stress and intonation.

*Certain: Anyway, there were **clear** divisions within the team, on a quite **personal** level.*
*Less certain: I would say it's **pro**bably something every manager should try …*

1 🎧 4.6 Listen to extracts from the talk. Match each extract (1–5) with A or B.

   A speculating with strong certainty _____

   B speculating with less certainty _____

2 🎧 4.6 Listen again and make a note of the words and phrases that helped you to decide, along with any pronunciation features.

3 🎧 4.5 Review the questions and then listen to the main part of the talk again. Work with a partner to answer the questions.

   1 What is the speaker's connection with the company he is talking about?
   2 What issue did the speaker identify regarding the physical environment?
   3 What did he do to solve the problem?
   4 What is the speaker fairly sure affects leadership values?
   5 What was the main issue with having two teams on the same project?
   6 How does the speaker describe the intervention in terms of risk?

E Critical thinking

1 Work on your own. What risks are there to a company in each of the following situations? Make a note of your ideas.

   • Weak management
   • A leak of confidential information
   • Unmotivated employees
   • Unrealistic deadlines

2 Share your ideas. Identify the two biggest risks for a company and present your ideas to another group. Justify your decision.

Critical thinking

Justifying decisions

We are often required to justify our decisions in academic or professional contexts. When we do this, we need to provide evidence to explain and support our decision. This evidence could include *experience*, *research*, and *proof of group consensus*.

For our justification to be effective, we need to avoid certain features of weak justifications, such as *circular reasoning*, *anecdotal evidence*, or *assertion of authority*.

1   Review the six justifications. Which three are effective? What is the problem with each of the other three?

   1   My tutor told me she always used to do the same thing.
   2   The decision is partly based on observations from a year's experience of working in this field.
   3   I have made this decision because I am the expert in this context.
   4   The most recent study in this area provides overwhelming support for this line of action.
   5   I understand the team. Therefore, the decision shows I understand the needs of the team.
   6   A vote was taken at last week's meeting to follow this decision.

2   Match the justifications in Exercise 1 with the six types listed in the box.

3   🎧 4.7 Listen to extracts from the lecture by the expert business consultant. Identify the decisions made in each extract.

Extract	Decision
____	To cut available time for projects
____	To make employment benefits more equal
____	To make people work together
____	To change location and, therefore, routine

4   🎧 4.7 Listen again and identify whether the decisions are well justified or not. What could strengthen them?

5   What possible justifications could there be for the following decisions?

   1   A college decides to restrict the opening hours of the library.
   2   Teachers decide students must arrive half an hour before an exam starts.
   3   A company decides to remove walls to make an open-plan office space.
   4   The management decides to organize a team-building day for all its staff.

Vocabulary development

Words for risk and conflict

1 Match the definitions with the verb phrases in the box.

| have a right to do   have no option   pose a threat to   put a stop to |
| run down   scare off   shake up   take something personally |

1 _____ to make someone feel so afraid about doing something that they decide not to

2 _____ to have no alternative choice or possibility

3 _____ to present a danger for others in the situation

4 _____ to change the way things are usually done

5 _____ to have justification for doing something

6 _____ to criticize someone in an unfair way

7 _____ to make something stop happening

8 _____ to feel that a failure is your fault and be upset

2 **Identify the phrases in the questions. Then make a note of your answers to each question.**

1 Why do people sometimes take things personally in a professional context?

2 What do most people feel they have a right to do at work?

3 Why do managers or leaders often say they have no other option?

4 How can a leader shake up a team that is not working effectively?

5 What scares people off from giving their real opinion in a group?

6 What should leaders put a stop to immediately on their teams?

7 What kinds of things pose a threat to the success of a project?

8 What kind of effect can running down team members have on the group as a whole?

3 **Discuss your answers to the questions above in a group.**

Academic words

1 Match the words in bold with the correct definitions.

1 **facilitate** (v)
2 **framework** (n)
3 **integrate** (v)
4 **intervention** (n)
5 **minimal** (adj)
6 **reliance** (n)
7 **underlying** (adj)
8 **undertake** (v)

a a very small amount
b an action taken, especially to prevent something from happening
c to make it possible or easier for something to happen
d the state of depending on a particular person or thing
e (facts, ideas, causes, etc., that are) not obvious or directly stated
f a set of ideas that you use when you are forming decisions
g to combine two or more things to make an effective system
h to agree to be responsible for a job or a project

2 Complete each sentence with a word in bold from Exercise 1.

1 A/an _____ for decision-making that everyone agrees with is essential.

2 _____ should happen as soon as there is a risk of a project failing.

3 Team members often have an over-_____ on a strong leader.

4 Managers are not the best people to _____ change; they need to bring in outside experts.

5 _____ problems need to be discussed openly for a project to succeed.

6 Effective managers _____ mechanisms for dealing with risk as well as success.

7 When team members _____ to do something, they need to fulfill their promise.

8 Most team goals can be achieved with _____ risk if everyone works together.

3 Choose the three sentences you most agree or disagree with in Exercise 2. Explain your choices to a partner.

Speaking model

You are going to learn about using hedging when you speak, using emphasis when you do this, and obtaining consensus. You are then going to participate in a discussion about the most effective way to manage conflict.

A Analyze

Review the discussion. Who does what, Jamil (*J*), Saud (*S*), or Marco (*M*)?

1 _____ Establishes the group task

2 _____ Recognizes the time limit

3 _____ Tries to establish a basic principle

4 _____ Suggests a more specific approach

5 _____ Refers to research supporting an alternative view

6 _____ Provides a counter argument

7 _____ Introduces other considerations

8 _____ Focuses on making a decision

JAMIL: So, just to remind ourselves, the topic we're discussing today is managing conflict. Our actual task is to decide how important it is for immediate intervention when problems arise in order to minimize risk of project failure.

SAUD: Yes, and we need to come to some kind of collective agreement on this so we can present our ideas to the group. We only have this session, so we should probably get started right away.

MARCO: Fine. OK … well, I think it can be argued that it's better to at least investigate underlying problems immediately, before they grow and pose a threat to the whole project. What does everyone think about that as our basic starting point?

SAUD: Well, OK, It **is** perhaps true that, overall, some kind of intervention will be needed, **but** I think it would be more effective to decide exactly when it happens based on the circumstances of the particular situation.

JAMIL: Yeah, Marco, I'm not sure I agree with your idea as a starting point. We've already looked at the specific cases of some team projects where the team had no option but to deal with their own problems. No intervention came from outside, so the team members simply had to take more responsibility for their own roles.

MARCO: It can be argued that in these cases that a lot of negativity had to be worked through, before the group started "performing." It could certainly be said in response that this was avoidable, if there had been intervention in their intragroup conflict earlier …

JAMIL: But it is certainly the case that external experts, for example, can have a rapid, positive effect on a team's performance. However, there is a cost to consider with this, and also the availability of someone with the right skills to be able to deal with complex situations.

SAUD: We can return to those points later. But, let's try to reach a decision on the main principle first …

B Discuss

1 Which stage might this group be at (forming, norming, etc.)?

2 What strategies and phrases used by each group member are effective?

Grammar

Hedging with *be*, *can,* and *could*

When speaking in an academic context, it is common to avoid making strong statements. This enables the speaker to discuss different ideas without committing to any particular theory.

Hedging with *be*

When hedging with *be*, use adverbs to show the degree of certainty of the statement.

certainly definitely   clearly probably   possibly   perhaps

Compare:

It is clearly
It is probably | true that group work is better.
It is perhaps

Hedging with *can* / *could*

It can be said that
It could be argued that | this view is not generally applicable.

"It" is often used as the subject in hedging sentences, referring to the later clause. The passive voice is also often used. Both these factors make the sentence seem more objective.

It could be said that **group work is the most popular way to work.**

1 Rewrite these sentences using hedging language.

  1 It is better to collaborate with others.

  2 Overall, having too many managers is a risk.

  3 This positive view of mavericks is not generally applicable.

  4 What we learn from them isn't applicable to most situations.

  5 Participation in teams can lead to intragroup conflict.

2 Compare your answers with the examples in the model. Were your sentences more or less certain?

3 Make hedging statements to show your opinion using the following key phrases. Compare them with a partner.

  1 working individually / working in groups

  2 collaboration / effective use of time

  3 working individually / creative

  4 group work / greater risk of failure

  5 dominant leader / increased conflict

Speaking skill

In a discussion, it is important to establish when the group reaches agreement.

So, are we all agreed that …
We all seem to be of the same opinion.

Different approaches can be taken to get everyone's view. These can be more or less structured.

Should we take a vote on that?
What does everyone think?

Group members need the opportunity to disagree and to express alternative views.

I'm not sure I agree with that. The way I see it is that …
I understand what is being said. However, …

If consensus cannot be reached, it is often a good idea to move the discussion on and return to the point later.

In the interest of time, let's move on.
We can return to this point later.

1   Match the purposes on the left with the phrases on the right.

1	establish agreement	a	We can revisit this issue later.
2	get everyone's view	b	The problem with that view is that …
3	disagree	c	We seem to be in agreement that …
4	move the discussion on	d	Let's see where we are with a show of hands.

2   🎧 4.8 Listen to three extracts from the Speaking model. Identify the speaker's purpose and make a note of the phrases used.

Speaker	Purpose	Phrases
1	_____	_____
2	_____	_____
3	_____	_____

3   Choose the two most important items for minimizing risk in group tasks. Then discuss your choices as a group. Attempt to gain consensus.

an achievable task   a challenging deadline   a strong leader
clear goals   friendship between group members

Pronunciation for speaking

Emphasis for hedging

When hedging, emphasis can be used to imply agreement or disagreement.

Implied agreement

Emphasis can be placed on the adverb or *can*.

It is *certainly* true that …
Despite some criticisms, it *can* be concluded that …

Implied disagreement

Emphasis can be placed on *be* or *could* and on the word signaling disagreement.

While it *could* be said that is the case, *most* people …
It *is* possibly true, *however* …
We *could* say that was the case, if it *didn't* …

1 🎧 4.9 Listen and read the extracts. Choose the correct verb form in the sentence below the extract to give the person's opinion.

   1 *It may be true that mavericks increase uncertainty, but they also apparently bring more creativity to a team.*

     Mavericks **can / cannot** make a team more creative.

   2 *These individuals, it has been argued, bring about anxiety and may sometimes threaten the status quo.*

     Teams **should / shouldn't** worry about some mavericks' presence.

   3 *While it could be said that risk is always a problem, many risky situations do tend to have their benefits.*

     Risky situations **are / aren't** always a bad thing.

2 🎧 4.9 Listen again and underline the emphasized words in the extracts from Exercise 1.

3 Work with a partner. Say the sentences from Exercise 1 and check each other's emphasis to imply agreement or disagreement.

4 Work with a partner. Make hedging statements with the sentences, and use emphasis to imply agreement or disagreement. Listen to your partner and check.

   1 Group conflict should be dealt with immediately.
   2 Overall, group work minimizes the risk of a project failing.
   3 This positive view of mavericks is not generally applicable.
   4 What we learn from mavericks isn't applicable to most situations.
   5 All decisions need to have strong justifications.

Speaking task

Have a group discussion about the most effective ways to minimize the risk of a team project failing.

Brainstorm

Review *Rule breakers, risk-takers* and *Managing risk*. Note points related to the topic of the discussion you are going to have. Review useful language.

Plan

Identify, discuss, and take notes on risks to successful group work.

Speak

Work in a group. Share your ideas. Discuss each risk identified and suggest various solutions. Try to obtain consensus in your group on the best solution.

Share

Work with a new group. Share the main points and outcomes of your group discussion.

Reflect

Using the information you learned throughout the unit, answer the questions.

1   How important is consensus in a group?
2   Is an element of risk present in everything we do?
3   What benefits does the presence of risk bring?

Review

Wordlist

MACMILLAN
DICTIONARY

Vocabulary preview

argumentative (adj)	maverick (adj and n)	scale (n) ***
assign (v) **	momentum (n) *	solitary (adj)
comprehensive (adj) **	preconception (n)	unconventional (adj)
confidential (adj) *	proportion (n) ***	weaken (v) **
distraction (n) *	pursue (v) **	
dysfunctional (adj)	risk-taker (n)	

Vocabulary development

have a right to do	put a stop to	shake up
have no option	run down	take something
pose a threat to	scare off	personally

Academic words

facilitate (v) *	intervention (n) *	underlying (adj) **
framework (n) **	minimal (adj) **	undertake (v) **
integrate (v) **	reliance (n)	

Academic words review

Complete the sentences with the correct form of the words in the box.

assurance	justification	minimal	underlying	undertake

1 There is no _____ for so many changes at the last moment!

2 Researchers study workers who work with _____ expenditure of energy and get less tired.

3 It wasn't an easy project to _____ in your first semester. Well done!

4 The _____ emotion here is not just reluctance to change – it's people's need to feel safe.

5 I will seek _____ from the board and let you know the result.

Unit review

Listening 1	☐	I can identify consensus in group speech.
Listening 2	☐	I can listen for speculation and degree of certainty.
Study skill	☐	I can study collaboratively.
Vocabulary	☐	I can use vocabulary for risk and conflict.
Grammar	☐	I can recognize and use hedging.
Speaking	☐	I can obtain consensus in spoken discussions.

Discussion point

Study the infographic about the global spread of companies, and answer the questions.

1 Do you eat at international chain restaurants? Why?

2 What makes a company successful globally?

3 What happens to the local competition when a successful outsider moves in?

4 What will happen with this trend in the next 20 years?

5 Which is a better description of this development: spreading or invading? Why?

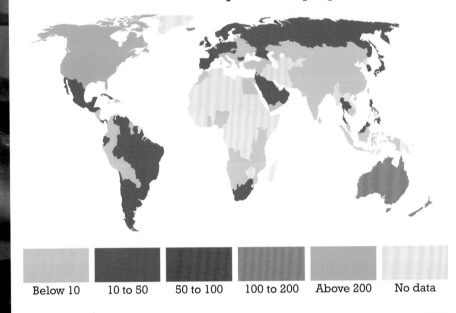

Fast-food outlets
by country and per person

Fast-food outlets per million people

| Below 10 | 10 to 50 | 50 to 100 | 100 to 200 | Above 200 | No data |

VIDEO

RIVER TAXI

Before you watch

Match the words in bold with the correct definitions.

1 **carjacking** (n)

2 **gridlock** (n)

3 **initiative** (n)

4 **in the works** (phrase)

5 **notorious** (adj)

6 **target demographic** (phrase)

a a specific group of customers

b an idea or opportunity

c famous in a negative sense

d planned

e the theft of a car while a person is in it

f very severe traffic congestion

UNIT AIMS

LISTENING 1 Listening to detect and repair lapses in understanding
LISTENING 2 Using extension materials to support understanding
STUDY SKILL Overcoming nerves

VOCABULARY Words for relationships
GRAMMAR Inversions
SPEAKING Drafting persuasive statements

A shoal of fish keeps together for safety.

While you watch

Watch the video and choose *T* (True) or *F* (False).

1 Cairo has a very efficient public transportation system. T / F

2 The traffic problems are caused by crime. T / F

3 The Nile river taxi company intends to extend its service for more people. T / F

4 The service can reduce travel times by more than 50%. T / F

5 Anyone can afford to use the service. T / F

After you watch

Discuss these questions in a group.

1 What kind of problems does your city have? Are they similar to the problems of Cairo?

2 What do you think are the problems of using the river as a means of transportation within a city?

3 What do you think can be done to reduce the migration of people to major cities?

4 What is your favorite city? Why do you like it?

5 What are the negative aspects of living in a large city?

The spread of English

A Vocabulary preview

1 Match the words in bold with the correct definitions.

1	**enhance** (v)	a	not supporting a particular side in an argument or disagreement
2	**exclude** (v)	b	relating to languages or words
3	**linguistic** (adj)	c	idea, knowledge, or understanding of something
4	**neutral** (adj)	d	happening in many places, or affecting many people
5	**notion** (n)	e	to improve something, or to make it more attractive or valuable
6	**obligatory** (adj)	f	describing something that must be done in order to obey a rule
7	**significance** (n)	g	the importance that something has because it affects other things
8	**widespread** (adj)	h	to deliberately not include someone or something

2 Complete the sentences with the words in the boxes.

excluded   linguistic   obligatory   widespread

1 Learning languages in an online environment becomes more _____ every year.
2 _____ knowledge helps you to understand a country's culture.
3 Knowing a country's language should be _____ for people going to live there.
4 Only one language should be used in the workplace; other languages should be _____.

enhances   neutral   notion   significance

5 The choice of language used in an international meeting has great political _____.
6 The _____ of the world needing an international language is wrong.
7 The choice of languages taught at school is not a _____ decision.
8 Speaking more than one language _____ your career opportunities.

3 Which of the sentences do you agree with? Compare your answers with a partner.

B Before you listen

1 How do you feel about each of these statements about learning English? Discuss your views with a partner.

1 I have no choice. It is obligatory.

2 I would feel excluded from a shared culture if I didn't learn it.

3 I feel fairly neutral about it.

4 It enhances my academic opportunities.

5 I love linguistic challenges and I'm learning several languages.

2 Which of these words are negative?

common   confusing   damages
destroys   dominant   widespread

3 Work with a partner. Predict statements that might be made about the role of English in the world using the six words in Exercise 2.

C Global listening

1 🎧 5.1 Listen to four speakers giving their opening statements in a debate. Number the main points in the order they are presented (1–8).

  _5_   Destroys other languages

  ___   Already dominating the world

  ___   Common language for many people

  ___   Damaging to the places it spreads to

  ___   Lives alongside other languages

  ___   Many different forms are confusing

  ___   Not obligatory, but a free choice to learn

  _1_   Widespread throughout culture

2 Review the main ideas. Which of the sentences below best describes how the debate develops?

a The speakers answer the moderator's questions with little or no time to prepare.

b The two sides of the debate give their views, but they also have the chance to interrupt or question the other side.

c The structure of this debate requires that all arguments of one side must be completed before the other side can begin to speak.

Listening for speakers' main points

Listening to detect
and repair lapses in
understanding

D Close listening

While listening, we can often recognize when we have missed some information. Make a note of the information given before and after the lapse, adding a question to indicate the type of information you think is missing.

adjective— "sp??"
... speaker uses this positively??

1st speaker: "English is a _____ language"

However, sometimes we are unaware that we have missed or misunderstood something. At the end of the listening, review your notes and identify unlikely or surprising information.

!!!
(181) countries with English as official language – CHECK!!!

Repair these lapses in understanding by asking questions or using reliable online sources to check the information later.

I'm missing some information. You said "English is a what language"?

What did you mean by "sprawling" exactly?

I'm not sure if I heard correctly. Did you say "181"?

You said "the official language," is that right?

1   Review the extracts from the students' notes. What lapse in understanding has the student identified in each: missing or surprising information?

1   2015– (10.5) billion worldwide speak English—*IMPOSSIBLE!!!*

2   Not helpful to learn Russian, Swahili, or French "not going to help anyone" — *does she really mean this?!!!!*

3   Local culture, language, customs, food, + (???) of how to live—*NEED TO CHECK*

4   Speaker says he "taught millions" —*WHAT?!*

5   2012: >21,000 articles, from 239 countries—_____% in English

2   🎧 **5.2** Listen to the extracts from the opening statements. Write the phrases used to repair the lapses and correct or add the information.

E Critical thinking

Discuss the questions in a group.

1   Which languages did you learn at school? Why do you think you learned these?

2   Which languages do you think should be taught at school? Why?

3   What languages are needed for the 21st century workplace?

Study skills | Overcoming nerves

Feeling nervous before giving a talk is a natural part of the process. To ensure the nervous excitement you feel has a positive impact on your performance, do the following.

- Prepare carefully—be confident about what you are going to say, and how you are going to say it.
- Memorize the opening—this will give you a strong start and make you confident.
- Make a conscious effort to relax before the talk.
- Be in the room before everybody else if possible. Smile and greet your audience members as they arrive.
- Accept your feelings, but see them positively, that is as excitement, rather than fear.

© Stella Cottrell (2013)

1 Discuss the questions in a group.

1 Which stage of giving a talk do you find most enjoyable? Why?

before the talk   during the presentation
Q&A at the end   after the talk

2 Which do you find most difficult to deal with? Why?

3 What strategies do you use to help yourself?

2 Read the study skill box. Then discuss the questions below in your group.

1 What can happen if the presenter doesn't use each of these strategies?

2 Which strategies have you used? How did they help?

3 Discuss and identify three more strategies to use during the presentation and two to use in the Q&A session at the end.

An unnatural spread

A Vocabulary preview

1 Match the nouns from the box with the correct definition.

density   distribution   diversity   ecology
extinction   habitat   modification   predator

1 _____ study of the environment and how plants, animals, and humans live together

2 _____ the way that something is spread over an area

3 _____ the amount of something in a place

4 _____ an animal that kills and eats other animals

5 _____ a small change to something

6 _____ the fact that very different people or things exist within a group or place

7 _____ the situation when an animal, plant, or language no longer exists

8 _____ the type of place that an animal or plant usually lives

2 Choose the correct noun to complete the sentence.

1 The rain forests are the natural **habitat / diversity / density** of over ten million species.

2 There is a growing interest in studying **predators / habitat / ecology** at universities.

3 The animal had no natural **distribution / extinction / predators**, so its population increased rapidly.

4 Several species of animal are close to **modification / extinction / density** and need protecting.

5 Any **modification / ecology / habitat** to a natural environment can have dramatic effects.

6 The **predator / modification / distribution** of certain animals globally has been affected by human transportation.

7 The population **extinction / density / ecology** of humans affects the animals living nearby.

8 The **modification / diversity / predator** of animal and plant life in places such as the rain forests is incredible.

3 Discuss the questions with a partner.

1 Think of a predator from your region of the world. What is its natural habitat?

2 What is the predator's population density and distribution?

3 Is the predator in danger of extinction?

4 Is there a lot of diversity in plant and animal life in general in your region?

B Before you listen

Use the additional materials provided with a lecture before, while, and after you listen to support and deepen your understanding.

Before you listen, review the materials to:

- familiarize yourself with the topic.
- predict the content of the lecture.
- check the meaning and pronunciation of key words.
- look up unknown terms for items featured in visuals.

While you listen, use the materials as a basis for your note-taking. Annotate and add further ideas and questions.

You will hear a lecture. Review the slide below with a partner.

1 Label the images. Use the words in the box and look up others you need.
2 Discuss your understanding of the title. Annotate the slide with your ideas.
3 Write three questions you think the lecture will answer.

bug   crab   fungus   rat   seed

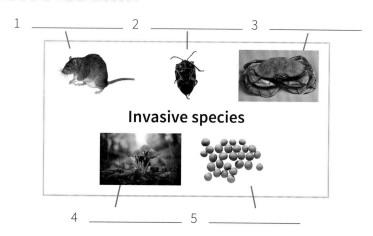

1 _____   2 _____   3 _____

Invasive species

4 _____   5 _____

C Global listening

🎧 5.3 Listen to the lecture and complete the outline for the talk.

- How do invasive species [1]_____?
  Intentional—Examples: swamp rat, [2]_____
  [3]_____ beetles, rats, plant seeds, [4]_____
- How do they become [5]_____?
- How can we [6]_____ the problem?
  Example from [7]_____ using apps

Annotating lecture slides

D Close listening

1 🎧 5.3 Listen to the lecture again and annotate the slides with more detail where you see ⊙.

Invasive species (or non-native) ⊙ Definition: animal, plant, fungus from elsewhere The predator advantage ⊙	**Getting to the habitat** Main method—human travel Intentional—for food, to breed, as pets Example—the nutria ⊙
Getting to the habitat Intentional Example—Chinese crab ⊙	**Getting to the habitat** Accidental—regularity of contact is important ⊙ Example—stink bug ⊙
Becoming a problem Natural evolution ⊙ vs. Unnatural spread ⊙	**Dealing with the problem** A technological solution to data gathering Where & how? ⊙

2 Review your notes with a partner. Add and adjust as necessary.

E Critical thinking

1 Work in small groups. Use your notes to prepare a 100-word opening statement to highlight the negative aspects of invasive species.

2 Listen to another group's opening statement. Note and give feedback on the strong points.

3 In your group, discuss the positive aspects of invasive species. Do they outweigh the negatives?

Critical thinking

Rhetorical devices

Skillful speakers use rhetorical devices to engage listeners and persuade them of their point of view. Rhetorical devices can use different features of language.

Content

- Metaphor links new ideas to a known concept to help understanding and promote familiarity.
- Sarcasm appears to praise but actually is critical.
- Hyperbole uses exaggerated language to emphasize a point.
- Rhetorical questions engage the listener but are answered for them.

Structure

- Parallel structures have the same grammatical pattern in both parts.
- Anaphora means repeating the same word or phrase at the start of successive sentences or clauses.

1 Read the extracts from *The spread of English* and *An unnatural spread*. Underline the rhetorical devices.

1 We will give you three reasons, three reasons that cannot seriously be denied, three reasons that prove our point beyond any possible doubt.

2 … What language are all these things in? You've guessed it, English.

3 I've taught English to millions of children in Spain and France, and it's amazing how they all benefited in so many ways.

4 In almost every country in the world, there is a recognition that to fail to learn English is to fail to join the international community.

5 Sorry, earlier you said that you taught millions? I'm not sure if I heard that right … you must be quite a teacher!

6 The disruption we cause could so often be easily avoided … we interfere with nature and it bites us back as often as not …

2 Match each extract with a rhetorical device in the box.

3 Discuss the extracts from Exercise 3 with a partner.

1 In your opinion, which uses of rhetorical device strengthen the person's argument? How?

2 Which weaken the argument? How?

Vocabulary development

Words for relationships

1 Read the sentences. Match the verbs in bold with the correct definitions below.

1 We need to take care of the situation so it doesn't **deteriorate** any further.

2 Invaders tend to either destroy or **displace** the inhabitants of the location.

3 Introducing new elements **disrupts** the natural process of development.

4 If we **eliminate** an animal's only predator, there's nothing to stop the population increasing.

5 It's often not clear at first which invasive species will **emerge** as the dominant ones.

6 In a natural evolution process, predators and animals that they hunt **exist** side by side.

7 With the growth of the travel industry, accidental invasive species **are on the increase**.

8 Many invasive species **present a danger** to the natural inhabitants of the location.

a _____ to interrupt something and prevent it from continuing by creating a problem

b _____ to be real, or to appear in the real world

c _____ to become worse

d _____ to be a threat to something

e _____ to take the place of someone or something

f _____ to be happening more often

g _____ to get rid of something that is not wanted or needed

h _____ to appear or become recognized

2 Make a note of your answers to the questions. Then discuss them with a partner.

1 What have you eliminated from your life recently?

2 What could present a danger to your future ambitions?

3 What has been on the increase in the news in the last few months?

4 What has deteriorated in your country in the last few years?

5 Who has emerged as an important figure in your country this year?

6 What kinds of things can disrupt our day-to-day routines?

Academic words

1 Match the words in bold with the correct definitions.

1 **arbitrary** (adj)
2 **distinction** (n)
3 **evolution** (n)
4 **hierarchical** (adj)
5 **investigate** (v)
6 **mature** (adj)
7 **migration** (n)
8 **policy** (n)

a the process by which people or animals move to another place
b a difference between two things
c no longer young; developed to have the good qualities of something older
d to try to find out the facts in order to learn the truth
e arranged according to importance
f a set of plans or actions agreed on by a group
g the way in which something gradually changes and develops
h not based on any particular plan, or not done for any particular reason

2 Complete the sentences with the words in bold from Exercise 1.

1 Governments need a clear _____ on how to protect local environments.
2 There is little _____ anymore between cultures, due to globalization.
3 _____ is a natural process; we shouldn't try to prevent animals (or languages) from dying out.
4 Governments will always organize themselves into _____ systems—it is how power works.
5 _____ of people around the world has always happened and always will.
6 The way the world is now is quite _____ because it is based on random events in the past.
7 It's only worth listening to _____ organizations and individuals; youth has little to offer.
8 We shouldn't try to _____ why problems exist; the focus should be on solving them.

3 Choose the three sentences you most agree or disagree with from Exercise 2. Explain your choices to a partner.

Speaking model

You are going to learn about forming inversions, using rhythm in rhetorical devices, drafting persuasive statements, and ordering arguments. You are then going to deliver an opening statement for a debate on the spread of chain stores around the world.

A Analyze

Read the opening statement to a debate. Answer the questions.

1 What is the motion of the debate?
2 Which side is the speaker on?
3 How many key arguments will she and her partner put forward in total?
4 How many key arguments will she put forward herself?

SPEAKER: The motion put forward today is that the spread of chain stores globally has a negative effect on local businesses. I ask you, can anyone really doubt that? Never have our streets been so full of stores from elsewhere. Not only has the presence of these invaders displaced our own local businesses, they have reduced diversity and are eliminating our culture. These predators are eating up the competition, and who is that competition? It's us, yes, that's right, me and you, and our livelihoods.

Today, we propose three arguments against this invasion—three arguments to consider, three arguments to educate, three arguments that prove that it could be so very different. But before all that, to be clear, let me ask you: just what is the problem with chain stores?

The problem with chain stores, dear audience, is this. More than 95% of store space on city streets and in out-of-town malls is occupied by these invaders. Let's stop and think about that. More than 95%. These invaders present a clear danger to local companies. At no time in history have there been so few local companies on our main streets. This sprawl is killing local business. Argument number one. I'll say it again: this sprawl is killing our—your—local business.

Argument number two? Argument number two concerns diversity. People assume globalization brings diversity. Not so. Think of the downtown where you live. Think of a downtown you've visited recently. Think of a downtown you've seen in a movie. What's the difference? Maybe the weather, but, I guarantee, not much else. Every store is the same, every product is the same, every choice has already been made for you. Only now are some of us waking up to the fact that we've been invaded and our culture stolen from us. Wake up and see that, too.

My debating partner will identify the third argument, but as you turn to listen to the opposing side's first opening statement, I can see already the realization on your faces of just how wrong this invasion is.

B Discuss

Discuss the questions in a group. Explain and support your views.

1 How strong is each argument she identifies?
2 What do you think the third argument will be?
3 What key arguments could the opposing side put forward?

Grammar

Inversion

We can create emphasis by using inversion. This technique places the verb before the subject to make the sentence sound more formal and also more noticeable. Compare the two sentences:

Had they originated there, this situation would not occur.
If they had originated there, this situation would not occur.

Inversion is used:

after frequency adverbs **seldom**, **rarely**, **never**.
Never before has a cultural change of this size happened so quickly.

after certain phrases with **no**.
Nowhere that it arrives does it improve life for the local people.

after certain phrases with **only**.
Only after humans started moving around the planet did this problem begin.

1 Put the words in the correct order to make sentences containing inversion. Check your answers with the Speaking model.

   1 been / never / our streets / have / so full of stores / from elsewhere

   _____

   2 the presence of these invaders / has / displaced / not only / our own local businesses, / they have reduced diversity

   _____

   3 there / at no time in history / have / so few local companies / been / on our main streets

   _____

2 Rewrite these sentences starting with the words in parentheses.

   1 There will never be a time when people decide to stay where they are. (at no time)

   _____

   2 People hardly ever choose familiar experiences when they can choose something more exciting. (rarely)

   _____

   3 We are realizing now that the spread of some companies means the extinction of others. (only now)

   _____

3 Do you agree with the sentences in Exercise 2? Explain your views to your partner.

Drafting persuasive
statements

Speaking skill

The aim of your persuasive statement is to convince people of your viewpoint. Employing a range of techniques will strengthen your statement, adding to its persuasive powers.

1 Clearly state the main viewpoint—presenting this as a fact provides a strong entry point.

2 Identify the key points—three is typically an effective number.

3 Appeal to reason with facts and figures—numbers are powerful and memorable.

4 Appeal to emotion—connect on a personal level with emotive language.

Remember, though the content of the statement is very important, the delivery will also affect how persuasive it is. Deliver your statement with confidence by doing the following:

- mark the script for pronunciation features.
- use an appropriate pace.
- practice, record, and review.

1 Read the Speaking model on page 92 and make a note of how the speaker covers points 1 to 4 in the skills box.

   1 _____
   2 _____
   3 _____
   4 _____

2 Work in pairs. Use your ideas from the Discuss section on page 92 to write an opening statement for the opposing team. Follow the steps in the skills box.

3 Practice the opening statement together so you can deliver it confidently. Give each other feedback on the delivery.

4 Change partners and deliver your opening statement again. How much have you improved? How?

Pronunciation for speaking

Rhythm in rhetorical devices

Effective speakers use pronunciation features to highlight and emphasize rhetorical features. Variation—changing speed, volume, pitch, and use of pauses—keeps your delivery interesting and listeners engaged.

- Pauses highlight important ideas or give listeners a moment to consider what has been said.
- Stress emphasizes the key words and contrasts the speaker wants to make.
- Pitch changes show the speaker's attitude to what is being said.

Be aware of the effect your voice has on what you say. For example, sarcasm is often expressed with a low pitch on the key word, with the word being lengthened. Make your voice work for you, as a deliberate choice, not against you.

1 🎧 5.4 Read the extracts containing rhetorical devices. Predict where the pauses, stress, and major pitch changes are and mark them. Listen and check. Then practice the sentences.

   1 It destroys local culture, local language, local customs, local food, local notions of how to live.
   2 Multiculturalism totally depends on it; without a common language, it cannot exist.
   3 The stink bug is now your neighbor, my neighbor, everyone's neighbor.

2 🎧 5.5 Listen and read the extracts containing rhetorical devices. Mark the pauses, stress, and major pitch changes. Then practice the sentences.

   1 What language are all these things in? You've guessed it, English.
   2 We will give you three reasons, three reasons that cannot seriously be denied, three reasons that prove our point beyond any possible doubt.
   3 In almost every country in the world, there is a recognition that to fail to learn English is to fail to join the international community.

3 Review the Speaking model with a partner. Identify rhetorical devices and mark the stress, pauses, and pitch changes on these. Take turns delivering sentences from this opening statement.

Speaking task

Make an opening statement in a debate about the spread of fast-food restaurants.

Brainstorm

Review *The spread of English* and *An unnatural spread* and the Speaking lesson.

- Read the debate motion below.

The spread of fast-food chains globally has a negative effect on local cultures.

- Work in pairs to brainstorm ideas for and against the motion.
- Change partners. Compare and add to your own list of ideas.

Research facts and statistics related to each of the ideas you identified. Review your answers and ideas about the infographic on page 80.

Plan

Work with a partner to plan your opening statements for or against the motion. Your teacher will instruct you on the side to take.

Speak

Pair up with two other students on the opposing side. Make your opening statements. Listen carefully to the opposing team's arguments and make a note of strong points.

Share

Work with a new group. Outline the key points put forward by each side. Compare the strengths of the other side's opening statements.

Reflect

Using the information you learned throughout the unit, answer the questions.

1 What are key elements of a strong opening statement?
2 In which situations should the spread of something be avoided, and in which can it be welcomed?
3 Will there be more or less diversity in the future?

Review

Wordlist

MACMILLAN
DICTIONARY

Vocabulary preview

density (n) **	extinction (n) *	obligatory (adj)
distribution (n) **	habitat (n) *	predator (n) **
diversity (n) **	linguistic (adj) *	significance (n) **
ecology (n) *	modification (n) **	widespread (adj) **
enhance (v) **	neutral (adj) **	
exclude (v) ***	notion (n) ***	

Vocabulary development

be on the increase	disrupt (v) *	exist (v) ***
deteriorate (v) *	eliminate (v) **	present a danger
displace (v)	emerge (v) ***	

Academic words

arbitrary (adj) *	hierarchical (adj)	migration (n) *
distinction (n) ***	investigate (v) ***	policy (n) ***
evolution (n) **	mature (adj) **	

Academic words review

Complete the sentences with the correct form of the words in the box.

evolution	facilitate	hierarchical	investigate	transformation

1   The effects of the new drug are still unknown—two teams _____ them at this research center.
2   Nasser replaced the old _____ structure with a more direct approach.
3   Over the summer, the campus was re-designed. It's a stunning _____!
4   The _____ of the writer's views can be traced in the diaries he kept.
5   The campus staff is here tonight to help _____ the big move.

Unit review

Listening 1	☐	I can listen to detect and repair lapses in understanding.
Listening 2	☐	I can use extension materials to support my understanding.
Study skill	☐	I can use methods to overcome nerves when speaking in public.
Vocabulary	☐	I can use words for relationships between things.
Grammar	☐	I can use inversions.
Speaking	☐	I can draft persuasive statements and order arguments.

6 BEHAVIOR

Discussion point

Study the infographic about spending habits, and answer the questions.

1 To what extent does the infographic reflect your and your family's experience of spending?

2 What methods do companies use to find out why we behave as we do?

3 How do companies use information about behavior? Who benefits?

4 Can all human behavior be explained?

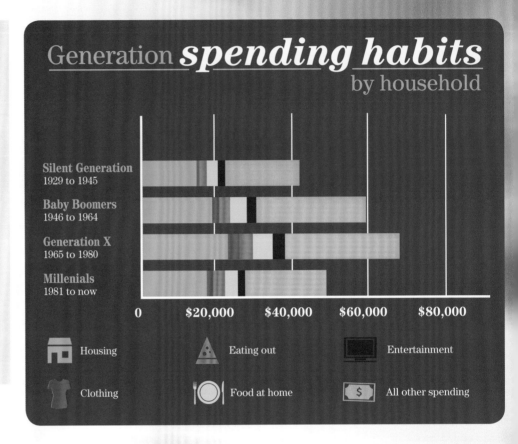

Generation **spending habits**
by household

Silent Generation 1929 to 1945	
Baby Boomers 1946 to 1964	
Generation X 1965 to 1980	
Millenials 1981 to now	

0    $20,000 $40,000 $60,000 $80,000

- Housing
- Eating out
- Entertainment
- Clothing
- Food at home
- All other spending

VIDEO

CHESS AND MEMORY

Before you watch

Match the words in bold with the correct definitions.

1 **breakthrough** (n)

2 **cognitive functions** (n)

3 **counterpart** (n)

4 **hippocampus** (n)

5 **impair** (v)

6 **onset** (n)

a a part of the brain associated with memory and emotion

b a person who has a similar function

c a sudden dramatic discovery

d mental activities that include acquiring information and memory

e the beginning of something

f to weaken or damage

UNIT AIMS

LISTENING 1 Concurrent note-taking and listening
LISTENING 2 Following abstract argumentation
STUDY SKILL Evaluating your questionnaire

VOCABULARY Phrases for navigating between questions
GRAMMAR Indirect questions
SPEAKING Conducting successful interviews

Taking part in a memory experiment.

While you watch

Choose the correct option to complete the sentences.

1 The increase in the number of Alzheimer's sufferers is due to **our modern lifestyles / people living much longer**.

2 Scientists believe playing chess can help prevent Alzheimer's because **chess players have to memorize complex routes / it provides mental exercise / mostly old people play chess**.

3 London taxi drivers are less likely to develop Alzheimer's because **they have to memorize various long and complex routes / they play chess**.

After you watch

Discuss these questions in a group.

1 What do you know about Alzheimer's?

2 What methods of improving memory do you know?

3 How do you try to memorize new words when you learn them?

4 What do you know about playing chess?

5 Which aspects of aging do you worry about?

Market research

A Vocabulary preview

1 Match the words in the box with the correct definitions.

deciding factor   determine   impulse   in retrospect
market research   move on   nutritional   obesity

1 _____ to control what something will be

2 _____ a sudden, strong feeling that you must do something

3 _____ considering something that happened in the past

4 _____ the process of collecting information about people's product preferences

5 _____ the thing that helps to make the final decision

6 _____ concerning food as something that keeps you healthy

7 _____ a condition in which someone is too fat in a way that is dangerous for health

8 _____ to stop doing or discussing something and do or discuss something different

2 Complete the questions with the words and phrases from Exercise 1.

1 What is a _____ for you when choosing which brand to buy?

2 Do you readily agree to take part in _____ surveys? Why / why not?

3 When choosing a snack to buy, do you look at the _____ information on the package?

4 What do you consider to _____ how much you spend each month?

5 Are there any products that, _____, you wouldn't have bought?

6 How often do you buy things on _____? Why?

7 How much are rates of _____ affected by the low cost of fast food?

8 How easy do you find it to _____ after wasting money on a product?

3 Interview your partner with the questions from Exercise 2.

B Before you listen

Work in a group. Someone stops you on the street to ask you some research questions. What would you expect the researcher to do?

- Ask questions
- Ask for your name and address
- Tell you how long it will take
- Tell you where they work or study
- Ask you to sign a confidentiality disclaimer
- Tell you the name of their professor

- Tell you the topic
- Give you a reward
- Tell you your answers are right or wrong
- Thank you for your time
- Offer to send you a copy of or feedback on the finished research

C Global listening

1 🎧 **6.1** Listen to two interviews. What do the researchers do from the checklist in *Before you listen*?

2 🎧 **6.2** Listen to the third interview. What does the interviewer not do that the others do?

D Close listening

Before listening

- Review the topic, check key vocabulary, and prepare your equipment for taking notes (paper, pencil, tablet, etc.).
- Sometimes (for example, for research) you may take notes on a particular form. Review the form you will use.
- Note how much space there is for answers, and consider if you will need more.
- Read the questions, headings, and sub-headings used to organize the notes on the form.

When listening

- Use headings and sub-headings to guide you as you listen.
- Note the key words and phrases, without trying to write complete sentences.
- Add annotations such as question marks to highlight points that need checking.
- Before finishing, review your notes and check that you have all the information you need. There may be an opportunity to ask questions at the end to complete your information.

1   Review the first questionnaire. Identify the sections and check vocabulary. Predict the words used in answers.

"Choices" Questionnaire   City University

Consumer planning

1   Why did you choose to come shopping here today?
   always come on [1]_____ */ get own* [2]_____ */ do*
   [3]_____ *shopping for* [4]_____
   [5]_____ *helps with groceries—then haircut or*
   [6]_____ */ "just what I* [7]_____ "

2   Did you buy anything unplanned?
   yes / sale / [8]_____ *+ sheets (needed the* [9]_____)

Budget allocation

3   How much money did you spend on the trip?
   about [10]_____—*groceries* [11]_____, *shoes* [12]_____

4   Do you have a specific budget when you go shopping?
   [13] ☐ *yes*   ☐ *no   other (please specify)* _____

Future intentions

5   When do you plan to come here again?   *same time next* [14]_____

Concurrent listening and note-taking

2   🎧 **6.3** Listen to the interview. Complete the questionnaire above.

3   🎧 **6.4** Listen to the second interview and make a note of the respondent's answers.

Doctorate Research, City University

Consumer planning

Why did you decide to come shopping today?
[1] _____

Do you have a specific time of the week designated for shopping?
[2] _____

Consumer intention

What stores did you visit? Why?
[3] Reasons—price / brand name / habit / location / sale / other
Location [4] _____   Reason [5] _____
How would you describe your purchase decision?
[6] ☐ rational   ☐ impulse   ☐ other (please specify) _____

E Critical thinking

Discuss the questions in a group.

1   What challenges do face-to-face researchers have to deal with?

2   What can they do to manage these challenges?

Study skills — Evaluating your questionnaire

Effective questionnaires produce quality research. Review your questionnaire before use to ensure you get the information you want, effectively and efficiently.

Time

- How long will it take to complete?
- Is every question necessary?
- Is the candidate told how long it will take?

Organization

- Are the instructions clear?
- Is the use of ranges (e.g., 1 to 5) consistent?
- Are questions in a logical order?

Questions

- Is there a range of suitable question types?
- Will the questions give the answers you need?
- Are there follow-up questions to clarify answers?
- Is every question a single question?
- Are the questions easy to understand?
- Will everyone understand the question in the same way?
- Are the questions too personal?
- Will the responses be easy to collate?

© Stella Cottrell (2013)

1   Work with a partner. Use the checklist in the Study skills box to review the questionnaires from the Close listening section. What improvements would you make?

2   Review the questions from different questionnaires. Check the two effective questions and identify the problem with each of the others.

> A not a single question   B difficult to understand
> C too personal   D difficult to collate

1   Can you tell me about your experience of shopping?

2   Which is your favorite store in this city?

3   How easy is it to go downtown and go shopping on the weekend?

4   If it weren't possible to acquire items needed in one location, what wouldn't you choose to do?

5   How often do shop online? Once a week or more / Less than once a week / Never

6   How much money do you earn?

3   Rewrite the problem questions from Exercise 2 so they are effective.

Asking the right questions

A Vocabulary preview

1   Match the words in bold with the correct definitions.

1 **convict** (v)	a having doubts about something that other people think is true or right
2 **distort** (v)	
3 **ethical** (adj)	b to suggest something is likely to be true without saying it
4 **imply** (v)	
5 **irrational** (adj)	c fair and reasonable; allowed by the law
6 **legitimate** (adj)	d to change something so that it is no longer true or accurate
7 **reinforce** (v)	
8 **skeptical** (adj)	e to make an idea, belief, or feeling stronger
	f done or happening without clear or sensible reasons
	g to prove in a court of law that someone is guilty of a crime
	h involving the principles used for deciding what is right and wrong

2   Complete the sentences using your own ideas.

1   I believe it is wrong to **convict** people who …

2   It is not **ethical** for companies to …

3   Information we see on … often **distorts** the truth.

4   Advertisements tend to **imply** that …

5   It is right to be **skeptical** about …

6   … often **reinforce** the wrong message.

7   It is very easy to make **irrational** choices when …

8   … is a **legitimate** use of …

3   Compare your sentences from Exercise 2 with a partner. How many of each other's ideas do you agree with?

B Before you listen

You will hear a lecture about memory, questions, and the mind. With your partner, discuss which of these is the best metaphor for human memory:

- a computer
- a leaky bucket
- a palace with many rooms

Compare and justify your ideas.

C Global listening

🎧 6.5 Number the main points in order.

Listening for main ideas

The lecturer …

___ compares two different ideas introduced previously.

___ describes a question type that gives the answer.

___ examines a question type that introduces new emotions.

_1_ explains the choice of lecture focus.

___ identifies a question type that suggests too much.

_2_ introduces two issues to be discussed.

___ justifies the argument against the mind-bucket comparison.

___ presents an argument against questionnaires.

___ provides a conclusion combining the two issues.

___ supports an argument with evidence from research.

D Close listening

Following abstract argumentation

Arguments are often presented in stages. Recognizing these stages helps the listener to follow and understand the line of reasoning and evaluate the conclusion reached by the speaker.

Assumptions—The speaker presents the premise of the argument, making one or more statements. The speaker may identify these explicitly as the argument.

Reasoning—Evidence is provided to support or refute the argument. The speaker can include reasoning for both sides, showing consideration has been given to more than one perspective. This often strengthens the eventual conclusion.

Conclusion—Having given the argument, and possibly summarized it, the speaker indicates his or her position.

Implicit assumptions are common in day-to-day life. In these cases, speakers, deliberately or not, include points they assume the audience believes, and provide no reasoning for these. Recognize these assumptions and then decide for yourself if you agree with the speaker.

1 🎧 6.5 Listen to the lecture again and decide if the statements are *T* (True) or *F* (False), according to the speaker. Correct the false statements.

1	The memory-computer analogy is accurate.	T / F
2	Questionnaires can distort people's answers.	T / F
3	It is easy to manipulate the type of answer given.	T / F
4	It is not possible to make people believe false things about themselves.	T / F
5	Politics and marketing use similar techniques.	T / F
6	Introducing doubt can change people's future decisions.	T / F
7	Leading questions are known to result in a reliable outcome.	T / F
8	People are influenced by suggestion.	T / F
9	It is not clear how the issues of the mind and questionnaires are linked.	T / F

2 🎧 6.5 Listen again and add further details to expand on each statement.

3 Work in pairs. Use the statements and your notes to answer the questions.

1 What two assumptions does the lecturer present?

2 What reasoning does he provide for (or against) each one?

3 What conclusion does he draw?

E Critical thinking

1 🎧 6.6 Review the final section of the skills box. Then listen to another extract and identify the three implicit assumptions.

1 _____

2 _____

3 _____

2 Work in small groups. Discuss the questions and the assumptions you noted.

1 Are they all reasonable assumptions to make in the circumstances? Why / why not?

2 How would changed circumstances alter your answers?

Critical thinking

Identifying loaded questions

Loaded questions contain assumptions that trap the respondent. The answer given will fit the interviewer's agenda, but may not reflect the truth.

Have you stopped spending too much money?

Possible answers: *Yes.* (I used to spend too much). / *No.* (I still spend too much.)

The interviewer's agenda is forcing the respondent to admit to spending too much money at some point. To escape the trap, the respondent needs to step outside the restricted range of answers to deny the underlying assumption.

I have <u>never</u> spent too much money.

Other examples of problem questions include:

Leading: *What were you doing at 3 p.m. on the day of the crime?*
Suggestive: *Don't you think people should work harder?*

1 Work in pairs. Discuss the problem questions used as examples in *Asking the right questions*, and identify the problem with each.

   1 Would you vote for this candidate if you knew that she was opposed by human rights groups?

   2 On the night of the murder, were you in New York?

   3 Don't you think that was wrong?

2 Review some of the questions from the interviews in *Market research*. Identify the loaded questions.

   1 Why did you choose to come shopping here today?

   2 Would you be more or less likely to buy this brand if you knew it was suspected of being linked to obesity?

   3 Did you buy anything unplanned?

   4 What choices did you make in terms of actual stores, and what were the determining factors in those choices?

   5 Would it affect the amount of this cereal you ate if no studies had been done on its nutritional value?

   6 If a new product was cheaper than this brand, would you change to the new brand?

3 🎧 6.2 Listen to the interviewer using the loaded questions and check. Then answer the questions with a partner.

   1 What kind of response did the interviewer get for each question?

   2 Was it a successful interview? Why / why not?

Vocabulary development

Phrases for navigating between questions

1 Read the extracts from *Market research* and complete the phrases with the words from the box.

> appear   basis   doubt   follow   make   stand   take   understood

---

"But I needed the sheets, anyway ... I'm not so sure about the shoes ..."

"I see. **To** [1] _____ **up on that,** would you mind telling me how much money you spent on this trip?"

"The shoes were 25 ... yes, about 120, 130."

"So **on the** [2] _____ **of** what you just said, **if I** [3] _____ **correctly,** you don't have a specific budget when you go out shopping ... is that right?

"No, no, I understand. I suppose they were a little bit of both, really ... I hadn't planned to buy it, but I'm glad I did—I don't regret it. I'm sure Flora will love it."

"OK, thanks, I'll just [4] _____ **a note of that** ..."

"I see. And would you say, in retrospect, that they were rational decisions, or more like impulse buys? I'm sorry, that sounds like I am **casting** [5] _____ **on** your choice ..."

"So, **it would** [6] _____ **that** you don't have a specific time of the week when you go shopping."

"I'd like to know **where you** [7] _____ **on** the brand in the picture. Would you be more or less likely to buy this brand if you knew it was suspected of being linked to obesity?"

"Obesity? Well, less likely, obviously ... **I** [8] _____ **it that** you have some evidence for that claim?"

---

2 Match the phrases from Exercise 1 with their function.

1 _____ clarifying understanding

2 _____ making something seem less certain

3 _____ recording information for later

4 _____ saying something seems to be the case

5 _____ stating something as the reason for the next thing

6 _____ stating that you think what you are saying is true

7 _____ continuing a discussion point

8 _____ stating what your opinion is about something

Academic words

1 Match the words in bold with the correct definitions.

1 **analogous** (adj)
2 **consultation** (n)
3 **contradiction** (n)
4 **equivalent** (adj)
5 **ignorance** (n)
6 **implication** (n)
7 **interpretation** (n)
8 **rational** (adj)

a the same size, value, importance, or meaning as something else

b a possible effect or result

c similar to another situation, so that the same things are true of both

d a discussion between people or groups before they make a decision

e a difference in statements that makes it impossible for all to be true

f lack of knowledge or facts about a situation or particular subject

g an explanation or opinion of the meaning or importance of something

h based on sensible, practical reasons rather than emotions

2 Complete the sentences with the correct form of a word in bold from Exercise 1.

1 _____ is not an excuse. We need to recognize gaps in our knowledge and fill them.

2 The best way to make difficult decisions is through _____ with everyone involved.

3 It can be difficult to make a/an _____ purchasing decision when surrounded by deals and offers.

4 We have to accept that life is full of _____, and try to deal with the conflicting information.

5 The way we learn is _____ to the way we fill a glass—we "pour" in the knowledge.

6 Much of what we say is open to _____: people understand things differently from each other.

7 All the _____ of a decision need to be analyzed before agreeing to it.

8 There is no _____ to having a face-to-face interview, if you want to get quality information.

3 Choose the three sentences you most agree or disagree with from Exercise 2. Explain your choices to a partner.

Speaking model

You are going to learn about using indirect questions when you speak, using stress in questions, and conducting successful interviews. You are then going to conduct an interview on student behavior.

A Analyze

Read the discussion. Answer the questions.

1 What is the purpose of the interview and how long will it take?
2 What does the interviewer (I) do to ensure the experience is positive for the respondent (R)?

I: Excuse me. Hello. I'm a student from the business college. I'm doing some research on spending habits of local residents, and I'd like to ask you a few questions, if that's OK. It will take about five minutes. Do you have time?

R: Oh, um, I'm not sure. How long did you say? I'm meeting someone in ten minutes.

I: Five minutes, maximum. I just have a few questions, and I'll make a note of your answers.

R: OK, then. Spending habits, you say. This should be interesting.

I: Thank you very much. So, first of all, would you say your spending habits have changed over the last year?

R: Well, yes, I would actually.

I: Why is that, do you think?

R: Well, I have just bought an apartment, and am paying a lot more each month on that. So, as a result, my day-to-day spending has been cut.

I: To follow up on that, could you identify how you feel about this change? Is "Pleased" or "Not pleased" the best summary?

R: Overall, I suppose "pleased" …

I: Can you tell me a little more?

R: Well, I'm happy with my overall circumstances—that is, owning my own apartment. But I miss having spare cash.

I: Thank you. OK, next question … I would like to find out where you stand on shopping malls. Do you ever visit the city mall?

R: Yes, I do.

I: Why is that?

R: Oh, well, to buy stuff, you know …

I: Can you give me more detail?

R: Well, I go there, I suppose when I have a lot of different stuff to get. It's convenient, you know, everything in one place …

…

I: … Well, those are all my questions. Thank you very much for your time. I really appreciate it.

R: My pleasure. It was interesting talking to you. See you.

B Discuss

Discuss the questions in a group. Explain and support your views.

1 What would stop you from being a respondent on a street interview?
2 What would encourage you to take part?
3 How useful is information from street interviews?
4 What makes the information more or less useful?

Grammar

Indirect questions

Indirect questions are used for different purposes in English. However, all indirect questions usually have the subject–verb order of a declarative sentence, and an auxiliary is not needed.

Polite questions

Indirect questions make a direct question softer and <u>more polite</u>. We do this by adding a *question head*, e.g., *Can you tell me …, I wonder if …*
Why <u>did you decide</u> to come shopping today?
Can you tell me *why <u>you decided</u> to come shopping today?*

Reported questions

The indirect form is used to report questions people asked. This usually involves a tense change and a pronoun change, too.
<u>Can we</u> *help?*
They asked *if <u>they could</u> help.*

1 Review the indirect questions from Listening 1 and 2. Identify the question heads and underline the main subject and verb.

   1 Can you tell me if you bought anything unplanned?
   2 Would you mind telling me how much money you spent on this trip?
   3 I'd like to know when you plan to come here again.
   4 I wonder if I could ask you a few questions?
   5 Can you tell me why you decided to come shopping today?
   6 Could you please explain what choices you made in terms of actual stores?
   7 I'd like to know where you stand on the brand in the picture.

2 Write the direct form of the indirect questions from Exercise 1.

3 Write the reported form of the questions in Exercise 2.

   Example: The reporter asked if the person could …

4 Find two examples of direct and indirect questions in the Speaking model.

5 Write indirect, more polite forms of these questions.

   1 How often do you pay with cash?
   2 Do you buy clothes online?
   3 Why do you choose particular brands?
   4 Would you like to reduce your spending?
   5 Has your spending pattern changed from a year ago?

6 Interview a student with your questions. Make a note of the answers.

Speaking skill

The questions

Successful interviews are well prepared and set up. First, plan your questions. Interviews use a variety of question types.

Open questions: Ask these to give the interviewee the opportunity to speak at length, but make sure you have sufficient space to make a note of all the key points of the answer.

What do you like about shopping online?

Closed questions: The yes/no or answer options often make these easy to answer, but limit the amount you learn from them.

Do you like visiting shopping malls?

Follow-up questions: Use these to help the interviewee expand on, illustrate, and justify their answers to open or closed questions.

Can you tell me more about that?   What's an example of that? Why do you say that?

1   Categorize the questions from the Speaking model.

   open   closed   follow-up

   1   Do you have the time?
   2   Would you say your spending habits have changed over the last year?
   3   Why is that, do you think?
   4   Is "Pleased" or "Not pleased" the best summary?
   5   Can you tell me a little more?
   6   Do you ever visit the city mall?
   7   Why is that?
   8   Can you give me more detail?

2   Ask your partner open or closed questions on these prompts. Ask a follow-up question for each one.

   credit cards   online shopping   saving   shopping malls

3   Work with a partner. Review the Speaking model interview.

   1   Practice asking the questions from the interview and then asking follow-up questions.
   2   Write two more questions, one direct and one indirect, on the same topic.

Pronunciation for speaking

Prominence in questions

Key words such as nouns and main verbs are usually stressed in English. In direct questions with a question word, this question word is stressed, along with the other key words. Yes / No questions tend to use rising intonation at the end to show it is a question.

What did you *buy?*   Did it *cost a lot?*

Polite indirect questions tend to be longer and have reduced stress on the question heads. Weak forms of the words link together and sounds are left out.

Could you tell me **how** *you* **decided**?

Listen for the key words within the reduced forms of these longer questions.

1 🎧 **6.7** Listen and read the questions from Listening 1 and 2. Identify the key stressed words.

    1 Can you tell me if you bought anything unplanned?

    2 I wonder if I could ask you a few questions?

    3 Can you tell me why you decided to come shopping today?

    4 Can you tell us how these biases can be avoided?

    5 To follow up on that, would you mind telling me how much money you spent on this trip?

    6 So on the basis of what you just said, if I understood correctly, you don't have a specific budget when you go out shopping … is that right?

    7 Could you please explain what choices you made in terms of actual stores, and what were the determining factors in those choices …

2 Review the questions. What types of words are missing in each?

    1 _____ did you first _____?

    2 Do you usually _____ or _____?

    3 Could you tell me how often you _____?

    4 _____ saying how much it cost?

    5 _____ how you choose which brand to buy?

    6 On the basis of that, _____ buy things on impulse?

3 🎧 **6.8** Listen and complete the questions with the missing words.

4 Practice asking and answering the questions with a partner.

Focus on giving prominence to the key words.

Listen to your partner asking questions and make a note of effective stress.

Give your partner feedback on the use of stress in questions.

Speaking task

Conduct a case study interview on student behavior.

Brainstorm

Review *Market research* and *Asking the right questions* and the Speaking lesson.

Work with a partner. Choose one of the following topics for your interview.

- Student spending
- Student saving
- Student shopping
- Student money management

Identify sub-topics of your chosen area.

Write at least ten interview questions. Focus on the question topic, rather than grammar, at this stage.

Plan

With your partner, review the questions and select eight to use in the interview. Edit the grammar of your questions, and include indirect question forms. Organize your questions into a logical order. Practice asking them.

Speak

Interview a student. Listen and make a note of the answers.

Share

Work with your partner again. Compare the outcomes of your interviews. Then report the key findings to the class.

Reflect

Using the information you learned throughout the unit, answer the questions.

1 What factors influence your behavior?
2 What benefits are there of researching people's behavior?
3 How many people's behavior must be studied before making generalizations?

Review

Wordlist

MACMILLAN DICTIONARY

Vocabulary preview

convict (v) **	impulse (n) *	nutritional (adj)
deciding factor (n)	in retrospect (phrase)	obesity (n)
determine (v) **	irrational (adj)	reinforce (v) **
distort (v) *	legitimate (adj) **	skeptical (adj)
ethical (adj) *	market research (n)	
imply (v) ***	move on (v)	

Vocabulary development

casting doubt on	it would appear that	to follow up on that
if I understood correctly	make a note of that	where you stand on
I take it that	on the basis of	

Academic words

analogous (adj)	equivalent (adj) **	interpretation (n) ***
consultation (n) **	ignorance (n)	rational (adj) **
contradiction (n) **	implication (n) ***	

Academic words review

Complete the sentences with the correct form of the words in the box.

analogous	contradiction	impose	interpretation	mechanism

1 I don't want to _____ rules on this debate club. Let's improvise.
2 The _____ of influencing memory seems complex, but really is simple.
3 Market research questions are _____ to court questioning in their effect on memory.
4 You can't seriously mean both these things at once. They're a _____.
5 The effectiveness of online questionnaires is open to _____.

Unit review

Listening 1 ☐ I can listen and take notes concurrently.
Listening 2 ☐ I can follow abstract argumentation in listening.
Study skill ☐ I can evaluate the effectiveness of my questionnaire.
Vocabulary ☐ I can use phrases for navigating between questions.
Grammar ☐ I can use indirect questions.
Speaking ☐ I can conduct successful interviews.

7 EXPANSE

Discussion point

Study the infographic about the value of space travel, and answer the questions.

1 Is space travel worth the money? Why / why not?
2 What should the goals of space exploration be?
3 Why do humans explore?
4 What will humans explore in the future?

Things we wouldn't have without space travel

Athletic shoes – NASA's research into suit construction technology means that many people today are able to wear a particular brand of sports shoe.

Camera phones – The JPL developed scientific quality cameras small enough for photography in space. 1/3 of all cameras now contain this technology.

Foil blankets – Light, strong, and very protective, these sheets were originally developed to protect spacecraft and astronauts. Now they are part of many emergency first aid kits.

Dust busters – NASA worked with a major company to develop the first of these light, portable devices to collect samples from the moon. Now many people have them in their home.

Wireless headphones – These were developed by NASA to give astronauts the freedom to move around without wires.

Freeze-dried food – NASA developed freeze drying as part of its research into space food. The technique reduces the weight of food to 20% of the original, but retains 98% of nutrients.

Glossary
NASA = National Aeronautics and Space Administration, the U.S. government agency responsible for science and technology developments in space
JPL = Jet Propulsion Laboratory, part of NASA and a U.S. government–funded research center, focusing on robotics in space

VIDEO

JUST LIKE ON MARS

Before you watch

Match the words in bold with the correct definitions.

1 **dome** (n)
2 **geological** (adj)
3 **isolation** (n)
4 **leap** (n)
5 **quarry** (n)
6 **simulate** (v)

a a rounded structure shaped like the top half of a ball
b a large step
c a place where rocks or minerals have been extracted from the ground
d a state of separation from others
e relating to the study of Earth's physical structure
f to imitate or copy something

UNIT AIMS

LISTENING 1 Identifying patterns in lectures
LISTENING 2 Listening to follow problems
STUDY SKILL Slide presentations

VOCABULARY Words for describing visuals
GRAMMAR Impersonal passives
SPEAKING Using visual data

The Milky Way, photographed on a clear night.

While you watch

Choose the correct option to complete the sentences.

1 The purpose of the experiment is to find out how astronauts will cope with **dealing with weightlessness / living and working on Mars / the journey to Mars**.

2 The simulation has been built **inside a volcano / on Mars / under a large dome**.

3 The crew have **limited contact with friends and family / delayed contact with the control team / TV and radio to keep up with the news**.

After you watch

Discuss these questions in a group.

1 What would you do if you were asked to go to Mars?

2 What do you think you would miss most while on the mission?

3 Describe the longest period of time you have spent away from friends and family.

4 Do you feel the money spent on space exploration could be better spent on improving conditions on Earth? Explain.

1 LISTENING

The new space race

A Vocabulary preview

Match the words in bold with the correct definitions.

1 **analogy** (n)
2 **conclude** (v)
3 **detect** (v)
4 **exacerbate** (v)
5 **payoff** (n)
6 **surpass** (v)
7 **vertical** (adj)
8 **weightless** (adj)

a the benefit that you get from doing something

b to decide that something is true after looking at all the evidence you have

c to become better or greater than something else

d having no weight, especially because of being outside Earth's atmosphere

e to prove something is present using scientific methods

f to make a problem become worse

g standing, pointing, or moving straight up

h a comparison between two situations that is intended to show similarities

B Before you listen

1 Work in a group. Brainstorm what you know about the two topics.

Developing space travel — **The new space race** — Finding new planets

2 Work with different students and share your knowledge.

C Global listening

1 🎧 7.1 Listen to students discussing their ideas for a presentation. How many of your ideas from *Before you listen* do they cover?

2 🎧 7.1 Listen again and number the main points (1–9) in the order each student mentions them.

___ Competitions encourage financial investment in space travel.

___ Distant planets are being discovered more easily now.

___ Early adopters can already buy an experience in space.

___ There are several methods for discovering the existence of planets.

_1_ The future of space research will focus on distant planets.

___ Investment in space travel follows other investment patterns.

_5_ Space travel is a financial issue.

___ The transit method involves measuring light.

___ There has been an improvement in the success rate of rocket launches.

D Close listening

Academic lectures often contain facts and statistical data that can be included in descriptions of patterns, as well as of trends and static numbers.

A pattern is a series of repeated events or actions that describes how things usually are.

When money is invested, the overall price comes down.

A trend is a change or development from how things usually are.

This number is increasing on a monthly basis.

A static number describes a single event.

It cost more than $1.5 million.

Presenters often use terms to make the statistical data approximate. This happens when the exact numbers are unknown or unclear, and also to simplify figures for the audience.

approximately   just under   just over   almost   more than   about

1 🎧 7.2 Listen to extracts from the discussion again and fill in each blank with one to three words or a number.

1 In successive years, the discovery rate has increased dramatically ... so in 2002, about [1]_____ new planets were discovered, and the transit method wasn't used, but by 2012, it was closer to [2]_____, and nearly [3]_____ of those discoveries used the transit method. Two years later, in 2014, it exceeded everyone's expectations of what was possible—nearly [4]_____ planets were discovered—mostly by using the transit method.

2 It's a way of detecting distant planets. What [5]_____ is measure the amount of light coming from a star. So, [6]_____ passes in front of a star whose light we are measuring, we [7]_____ less light coming in, because the planet blocks some of it. But when a planet passes out of the star's way, the light we can measure [8]_____ normal. Then the planet [9]_____, after a while, and the light we measure dips again. When a planet passes between the star and the Earth, this is called the "transit."

3 So for example, the Ansari X Prize competition, which offers a prize worth $[10]_____, has resulted in over $100 million of private space development.

4 ... SS2, which is an [11]_____-meter rocket glider that will take [12]_____ people under the mother ship, which is a [13]_____-meter wingspan aircraft.

5 Then the routine the trip will follow is this: The aircraft will take them up to approximately ¹⁴_____ meters, and then it will separate and go up to about ¹⁵_____ kilometers on a parabolic flight. That's when they'll have their five minutes of fun … and then they'll come down to just over ¹⁶_____ meters before gliding back to Earth.

6 And another major player I'm going to talk about is SpaceX. They managed to secure a $¹⁷_____ contract with NASA.

7 They're getting ¹⁸_____, year after year. So, let's see … ah yes, in 2012, SpaceX ¹⁹_____ two launches—and one of them was a partial failure. In 2014, the number of launches ²⁰_____ and all six were successful. In 2016, the number of rockets launched ²¹_____ to nine rockets, and only one of these was lost.

2 Discuss the extracts in Exercise 1 with a partner. What does each extract represent—a pattern, trend, or static figure? What language features indicate this?

E Critical thinking

Work in a group. You are going to select and organize information for the *Space race* presentation.

1 Evaluate the information discussed by the two students. Discuss each of the areas in relation to the questions.

   a What were the main points?

   b What are the pros and cons of focusing on this information alone in the presentation?

2 Think creatively.

   a What are different ways you could organize the presentation?

   b How could the information from the three parts of the discussion be combined into one presentation?

   c What other information or topic areas could be included?

3 Make a decision.

   a What information from the discussion would you include in the presentation?

   b How would you organize it?

   c What other information or topic areas would you include?

Study skills   Slide presentations

Effective slides provide valuable visual support for the information you are presenting in two ways: the slides help the audience to understand, and they help the speaker to give a stronger presentation.

For maximum effect, keep the slides simple by doing the following:

- use large text (at least 28 point) and a clear font style.
- use bullets and short sentences.
- label visuals carefully—minimally but clearly.
- limit video to two minutes.
- limit the use of special effects (e.g., sounds and animation).
- have a uniform approach (e.g., all slides enter from the same side).

Remember, your spoken presentation is the focus—the slides are just the support.

- Prepare the slides *after* establishing the main points of your presentation.
- Include one slide for every two to three minutes of presentation only.

© Stella Cottrell (2013)

1   Discuss each bullet point from the Study skills box with a partner. What would happen if the presenter did not follow each piece of advice?

2   Use the Study skills points to evaluate the slides used by the first speaker from *The new space race*. Annotate the slides to show how you would edit them.

In successive years, the discovery rate has increased dramatically. In 2002, about 40 new planets were discovered, and the transit method wasn't used, but by 2012, it was closer to 140, and nearly 100 of those discoveries used the transit method. Two years later, in 2014, nearly 1,000 planets were discovered, mostly by using the transit method. So, it can be concluded that the transit method is now the astronomer's favorite.

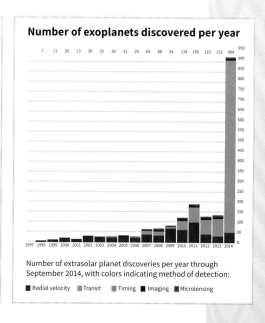

Number of exoplanets discovered per year

Number of extrasolar planet discoveries per year through September 2014, with colors indicating method of detection:
■ Radial velocity ■ Transit ■ Timing ■ Imaging ■ Microlensing

3   Review the script from the second speaker and design two slides to support the presentation.

Mapping the world

A Vocabulary preview

1 Match the words in bold with the correct definitions.

1	**accommodate** (v)	a	not changing frequently and not likely to suddenly become worse
2	**hazard** (n)	b	anything that encourages something to happen, develop, or improve
3	**interaction** (n)	c	something that could be dangerous
4	**navigation** (n)	d	the activity of being with and talking to other people
5	**parallel** (adj)	e	a way to find and follow a path through a difficult place
6	**source** (v)	f	to locate and obtain something from a particular place
7	**stable** (adj)	g	to consider and include something when you are deciding what to do
8	**stimulus** (n)	h	describing lines that are the same distance apart at every point along their whole length

2 Complete the sentences with the words in bold from Exercise 1.

1 Computer systems nowadays are completely _____.

2 Face-to-face meetings are better than online meetings because they allow more _interaction_ between the people involved.

3 Soon our planet won't be able to _accommodate_ everyone, so we need to expand into space.

4 Technology has made _navigation_ so easy that people are losing the ability to find their way around new places without it.

5 The main _stimulus_ for space travel is the human desire to discover new things.

6 The possibility of bringing back new diseases is a major _____ of space travel.

7 Two lines that are _____ can never meet.

8 Employers need to _____ new talent to ensure their companies are successful.

3 Which sentences are true in your opinion? Compare your ideas with a partner.

B Before you listen

1 Work in pairs. Choose one of the topics and discuss it in relation to the questions.

    Topic 1: Traffic   Topic 2: Maps

  1 What is your personal experience with this topic?

  2 What do you know about this topic on a more academic level?

  3 What do you think these concepts mean in relation to the topic?

Topic 1:	Topic 2:
Traffic control	Map making
Density, speed, and flow	Crowdsourcing

2 Work with a pair that discussed the other topic. Share your discussion, knowledge, and experience with the topic you focused on.

C Global listening

1 🎧 7.3 Listen to the lecture. What information from your discussion is included? Make a note and compare with your partner after listening.

Listening to confirm predictions

2 🎧 7.3 Listen to the lecture again. Number the stages (1–11) as the lecturer goes through them.

- Discuss flow ___
- Outline the theme of the lecture _1_
- Discuss speed ___
- Describe traffic flow in basic terms ___
- Discuss density ___
- Outline problems with a new form of mapping ___
- Move on to the topic of maps _8_
- Discuss the concept of maps ___
- Discuss a new form of mapping ___
- Present the concept of a time-space diagram ___
- Describe traffic flow in detail ___

D Close listening

Listening to follow
mathematical or scientific
problems

Mathematical and scientific lectures can be complex, containing high-level terms and concepts. Prepare thoroughly before listening by checking key terms and concepts. Strategies for listening include:

- Make a note of numbers and terms you hear.   100 cars per 1 km
- Use mathematical and scientific symbols in your notes.   >
- Note the name of the concept so you can research it later.   "flow"
- Listen for definitions of concepts.   *this means   that is to say   refers to*
- Use diagrams in your notes—copy the speaker's and/or create your own.
- Note when you don't understand a point so you can check it later.

When information is complex, focus on noting it down rather than trying to understand it during the talk. You can review it later.

1 🎧 7.4 Listen to extracts from the talk. Choose the problem outlined.

1 There is an issue with density when **not enough cars are produced / too many cars are in use**.

2 Restricted flow is a problem when **traffic conditions are not stable / there are fewer than 50 cars per minute**.

3 Speed variables of all vehicles **cannot be measured / are too specific.**

4 There is an issue of inaccuracy with **the "space mean speed" method / the "time mean speed" method**.

5 The issue with mapping is **the lack of change over the years / the changeable nature of geography**.

6 Locating the police **could mean police stations are not protected / could put the officers in danger**.

7 Crowdsourcing map information could **be dangerous for the people involved / lead to inaccurate maps**.

2 🎧 7.4 Listen again and make notes on the details of each problem.

E Critical thinking

Work in small groups. Discuss each set of questions.

Traffic 1 What are the day-to-day results of traffic problems?

2 What are the solutions for these?

Maps 1 What are the root causes of an absence of quality maps?

2 How can these be dealt with?

Critical thinking

1   Review the visuals
    with a partner.
    What problems can
    you identify?

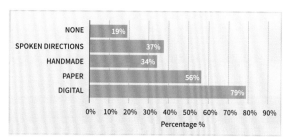

Chart 1

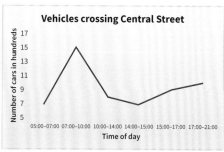

Chart 2

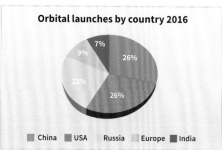

Chart 3

Identifying problems in visuals

Charts, graphs, diagrams, and tables are used to enhance and support
a presentation. Design your visuals for maximum positive impact and
informative value. Analyze your visuals, and those of presenters you watch,
to check that the visuals do not mislead or misinform.

- Choose the right graph to produce accurate, meaningful visuals.
- Remove unnecessary, repeated information, e.g., symbols
- Ensure consistent and clear use of color.
- Consider the position of labels.
- Use evenly spaced dates in a time series.
- Start bar graph values at zero.

2   Read the skills box. Analyze the visuals in Exercise 1 again and identify an
    example of each of the six issues from the box. What problems with data
    interpretation do these issues cause?

3   Discuss and design appropriate visuals for the following sets of information.

Set 1

**The diameter of the
four smallest planets in
the solar system (to the
nearest 500 km)**

Earth: 13,000 km
Venus: 12,000 km
Mars: 7,000 km
Mercury: 5,000 km

Set 2

**Mode of transportation
used by local commuters
in 2017**

Car   21%
By foot   11%
Bus   20%
Metro   31%
Bicycle   9%
Motorcycle   2%

Set 3

Public view of spending on space exploration

	2000	2005	2010	2015
Too much	51%	49%	35%	31%
Too little	12%	16%	19%	24%
About right	37%	35%	46%	45%

Vocabulary development

Words for describing visuals

1 Match the words in the box with the parts of the chart.

> curve   data point   label   series data
> unit of measurement   x-axis   y-axis

4 _____

5 _____

3 _____

2 _____

6 _____

7 _____

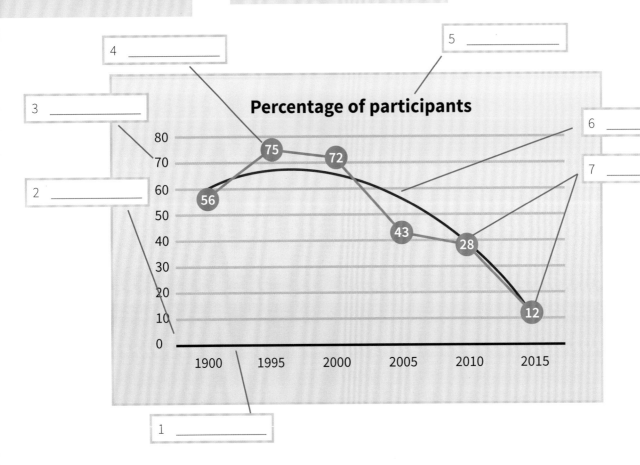

Percentage of participants

1 _____

2 Review other charts in the unit and label them with different parts above.

Academic words

1   Match the words in bold with the correct definitions.

1   **deduce** (v)
2   **exceed** (v)
3   **formula** (n)
4   **guidelines** (n)
5   **logic** (n)
6   **principle** (n)
7   **successive** (adj)
8   **validity** (n)

a   the way someone connects ideas when explaining or giving a reason

b   a basic belief that has a major influence on the way something is done

c   a plan or method for dealing with a problem or achieving a result

d   the extent to which something is logical, reliable, and correct

e   coming or happening one after another in a series

f   to be greater than a number or amount

g   to know something as a result of considering the evidence you have

h   official instructions or advice about how to do something

2   Choose the correct word for the collocations.

1   **deduce / exceed** expectations
2   apply **validity / a formula**
3   follow **guidelines / successive**
4   see the underlying **guidelines / logic** in something
5   understand a basic **principle / validity**
6   hear two arguments with equal **validity / formula**
7   **deduce / exceed** something easily
8   do the same thing for three **successive / formula** years

3   When did you last do the things from Exercise 2? Choose three, make notes about them below, and explain the situations to your partner.

1   _____
    _____
2   _____
    _____
3   _____
    _____

Speaking model

You are going to learn about using impersonal passives when presenting, pronouncing numbers and math and science symbols, and using visual data. You are then going to give a presentation using visual data on people's opinion on space exploration.

A Analyze

Read the discussion. Complete the visuals the student is presenting.

So, turning now to the results of our survey, this first chart shows the respondents' first choice of transportation for their trips to and from work or school. It can be seen there is clear preference for public transportation, with just over 60% opting for the bus or metro. That's three out of five people relying on public transportation for their daily commute. This supports our overall argument that public transportation needs to be a priority for governments. The bus just beats the metro, with 32% of respondents choosing this, compared with 29% opting for the metro. The least popular options are car and taxi, with only 4% and 1% of respondents, respectively, using these methods of transportation. To put that in context, that would be this small audience in this room in cars, with the rest of the 1,000 students at this school opting for alternative, more environmentally friendly methods. Free options for the daily commute occupied the middle ground, with 13% of respondents using the bicycle and a healthy 21% opting to walk.

Moving to the next set of data now. We wanted to investigate any identifiable trends over the past four years, and then to explore possible reasons behind these. Taking trips made by foot first. It can be clearly seen from our data that these trips are in decline. The highest data point came in 2015, with 34% of respondents opting to walk. This was a slight increase, from 30% in 2014. However, this had dropped to only one in four people in 2016, and the following year, to approximately one in five.

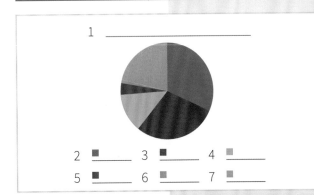

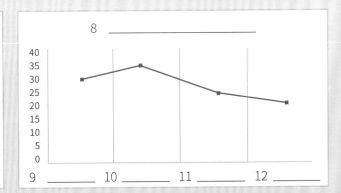

B Discuss

Discuss the questions in a group. Explain and support your views.

1 What informs people's choice of mode of transportation?
2 What would you do to improve traffic flow where you live?
3 Are your suggestions likely to happen in the next five years? Why / why not?

Grammar

Impersonal passive

We use the impersonal passive to present information in a more formal way. The structure is used with verbs of perception such as *think*, *know*, *say*, *understood*, *expect*, *see*, and *conclude*.

It is known that competition helps investment.
It can be seen that this method is the most successful.

The first part of the sentence is passive and the second part remains the same as the original base sentence.

It is expected that rocket launches will increase.
Rocket launches will increase.

1 🔊 **7.5** Identify the errors in the impersonal passive forms from Listening 1 and 2. Listen and check.

   1 So, it can concluded that the transit method is now the astronomer's favorite.

   2 It can be see that competitions can be used as drivers for investment.

   3 It generally accepted that "space mean speed" is the better option.

   4 Looking at the chart, it can clearly been expected that traffic flow will be far from predictable.

   5 It is know that any mapping of its edges is a temporary exercise.

2 Find the examples of the impersonal passive form in the Speaking model.

3 Put the words in the correct order. Then check the impersonal passive sentences.

   1 government spending / it / said / want more / that people / is / on transportation

   2 wants / public money / no one / going to / to see / waste

   3 will / the desire / humans / have / always / to explore

   4 can / it / that public opinion / known / is / on such issues / quickly change

   5 would like / it / seen / to prioritize / that most people / can be / scientific research

   6 mapped / has / by / the entire world / been / humans

4 Rewrite the active sentences from Exercise 3 in the impersonal passive form.

Speaking skill

Using visual data

For an effective presentation, display your data in visual form while presenting it to the audience. However, you need to go further than only displaying the information.

1 **Refer to the visuals.**

This next chart shows this clearly.   This illustrates my point …

2 **Describe the information.**

On the left you can see …
The highest point on the line graph shows us that …

3 **Put the numbers in context.**

That's the equivalent of …   It is X, which is the size of three elephants …

To enhance your presentation of numbers:

- round numbers up to keep them easy to understand, and use words such as *approximately.*

- look for opportunities to use alternative expressions, e.g., *63% or, to put that another way, three out of five.*

- avoid using too many numbers together.

1 **7.6** Listen and complete the phrases used to refer to visuals from Listening 1 and 2 and the Speaking model.

1   The _____ shows the number of exoplanets discovered, and the _____ shows the year.

2   You can see the basic _____ here.

3   To _____, that would be about $12,000 today.

4   On _____, we can see three basic principles.

5   This _____ my point.

6   This _____ this clearly.

7   The reason is a little complicated, but this _____.

8   Time _____ on the x-axis, and distance _____ on the y-axis, as you can see.

9   To get an idea, look at _____.

10   So, to _____, there's a social cost to this type of map.

2 Match the phrases from Exercise 1 with the three categories in the skills box. Then practice saying them.

3 Work in pairs. Choose slides from this unit (e.g., from the Listening 1, Critical thinking, or Speaking model sections). Deliver a one-minute presentation using phrases to refer to them.

Pronunciation for speaking

Pronouncing numbers and math and science symbols

Present numbers and math formulas effectively by using pronunciation features to engage the audience and highlight key information. Prepare before the presentation by checking pronunciation of key mathematical and scientific terms.

≥ *"greater than or equal to"*

°C *"degrees Celsius"*

approximately   "aPPROXimately"

When you present numbers, use:

- an engaging tone, which has pitch changes, stresses key words, and is not monotonous.
- pauses before and after key terms and numbers.
- correct word stress in multi-syllable words.

1 🎧 **7.7** Work with a partner. Discuss how to say the following symbols, abbreviations, and numbers. Listen and check. Then practice with your partner.

1 %	3 km	5 1/3	7 0.4	9 2.7
2 °F	4 kg	6 2/3	8 0.006	10 8.1 million

2 🎧 **7.8** How do you say these math symbols? Discuss them with a partner. Listen and check. Then practice with your partner.

1 ±	3 ≈	5 ≤
2 ≠	4 ≉	6 ∴

3 Combine numbers and symbols or abbreviations. Ask your partner to say them. Are the key words stressed and is the tone engaging?

$x \leq 5$

"x is less than or equal to five"

4 Complete the sentences by contextualizing the numbers or using alternative expressions. Practice presenting the information to a partner.

1 It is 50°C. To put that into context …

2 It weighs 800 kg, which is the …

3 That means more than 80%, or to put that another way …

4 The total is 7 billion—that's the equivalent of …

Speaking task

Present visual data to explain the results of a survey on public transportation in your city.

Brainstorm

Review *The new space race* and *Mapping the world* and the Speaking lesson.

Work with a partner.

- Identify the area of public transportation in your city you would like to research. Use an idea from the list or of your own.
  - spending on buses, trains, trams, bicycle infrastructure
  - students' preferences and habits when commuting
  - awareness of current public transportation situation
- Construct a survey containing four to six questions.
- Conduct the survey.

Plan

Review, organize, and analyze the survey responses. Create visual data charts to present some of your findings.

Prepare and practice the presentations of the data.

Speak

Work in with another pair. Present your data to the other students. Take notes while you watch the other presentations, and ask questions to clarify at the end.

Share

Discuss the presentations. Share your notes with the presenters. Are the notes accurate? Identify the information that was delivered effectively.

Reflect

Using the information you learned throughout the unit, answer the questions.

1 What are the benefits of using numbers in presentations?
2 How good is public transportation in the place where you live, according to the presenters?
3 Is spending on space exploration more or less reasonable than spending on new forms of transportation in cities?

Review

Wordlist

MACMILLAN
DICTIONARY

Vocabulary preview

accommodate (v) *	interaction (n) **	stimulus (n) **
analogy (n) *	navigation (n) *	surpass (v)
conclude (v) ***	parallel (adj) **	vertical (adj) **
detect (v) **	payoff (n)	weightless (adj)
exacerbate (v)	source (v)	
hazard (n) **	stable (adj) **	

Vocabulary development

categories	label **	x-axis
curve **	series data	y-axis
data point	unit of measurement	

Academic words

deduce (v)	guidelines (n) **	successive (adj) **
exceed (v) **	logic (n) **	validity (n)
formula (n) **	principle (n) ***	

Academic words review

Complete the sentences with the correct form of the words in the box.

deduce   exceed   reliance   sphere   validity

1   Our city worked hard to reduce its _____ on fossil fuels.
2   In the public _____, these kinds of statements are usually rare.
3   Many researchers published different results, questioning the paper's
    _____.
4   The sum of all the charity money will _____ last year's total.
5   The detectives looked through the data and were able to _____ the
    suspect's motive.

Unit review

Listening 1   ☐   I can identify patterns in lectures.
Listening 2   ☐   I can listen to follow problems.
Study skill   ☐   I can improve my slide presentations.
Vocabulary   ☐   I can use words to describe and refer to visuals.
Grammar   ☐   I can use impersonal passives.
Speaking   ☐   I can use visual data.

Discussion point

Study the infographic about replacing common household items, and answer the questions.

1 How much of the information in the infographic were you familiar with?

2 Why do people change items less often than recommended?

3 Why do people change items more often than needed?

4 What are the wider benefits and drawbacks of replacing items (e.g., economic, environmental)?

When is it time to replace ...?

Bathroom

Toothbrush: 3–4 months, but more frequently if you are a hard brusher.

Bath sponge: Every month, but only this infrequently if you let the sponge dry after use. Tip—don't keep it in the shower.

Bedroom

Mattress: 5–10 years. Do you sleep better away from home? If you wake up tired every morning in your own bed, it may be a sign that you need to change a mattress.

Pillows: 6 months. Supporting your head every night, these fill quickly with bugs, body oil, and dead skin cells.

Kitchen

Frying oil: Use it three times and then throw it out. Replace sooner if you detect changes in color or odor.

Spices: Ground spices, every 2–3 years; whole spices every 3–4 years.

Sports equipment

Yoga mat: 6–12 months, sooner if there are holes or smells.

Running shoes: 300–500 miles, sooner if you are a hard-core marathon runner.

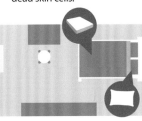

VIDEO

A JOB FAIR

Before you watch

Match the words in bold with the correct definitions.

1	**constraints** (n)	a	attach to
2	**diligent** (adj)	b	being careful and conscientious in work
3	**latch on to** (v)	c	limitations or restrictions
4	**proximity** (n)	d	nearness
5	**segregation** (n)	e	the separation of different types of people
6	**unchaperoned** (adj)	f	without supervision

UNIT AIMS

LISTENING 1 Understanding non-standard accents
LISTENING 2 Understanding rapid, colloquial speech
STUDY SKILL Lecturers' varied approaches

VOCABULARY Phrases for discussions
GRAMMAR Past modals in conditionals
SPEAKING Preparing and asking questions

A busy newsroom in a media company.

While you watch

Watch the video and choose *T* (True) or *F* (False).

1   Not many Saudi women wish to work.   T / F
2   It is difficult to employ Saudi women because they cannot work close to unmarried Saudi men.   T / F
3   Saudi women wish to work in order to help support their families.   T / F
4   Private companies don't like employing Saudi women.   T / F
5   Muna Abusulayman thinks it's more important to get a job than to wait for the perfect job.   T / F

After you watch

Discuss these questions in a group.

1   What did you learn about the roles of women in Saudi Arabia?
2   What do you think about Muna Abusulayman's advice?
3   How would you feel about working for free in order to gain the experience you need for a better job?
4   What would be your ideal job?

All change, please

A Vocabulary preview

1 Match the words in bold with the correct definitions.

1	**campaign** (n)	a	to get rid of something
2	**cutthroat** (adj)	b	a series of actions intended to produce political or social change
3	**directive** (n)	c	when you see someone or something for a moment only
4	**do away with** (v)	d	an official order
5	**feasible** (adj)	e	weak or easy to hurt physically or mentally
6	**glimpse** (n)	f	describing situations when people behave unfairly to get an advantage
7	**infrastructure** (n)	g	the set of systems within an organization that affect operations
8	**vulnerable** (adj)	h	possible or likely to succeed

2 Complete the questions with the words in bold from Exercise 1.

1 Have you been part of a _____ to encourage people to reuse rather than replace items?

2 How would you improve the _____ of the place you work or study?

3 Should a company _____ be followed without question?

4 What household items could you happily _____?

5 What makes companies or people _____ in the modern world?

6 Is it _____ to expect people to change household goods so often?

7 Do businesses do better in a _____ environment, or would cooperation be more effective?

8 Is a _____ of a better future enough to get people to accept change?

3 Work with a partner. Discuss your answers to the questions.

B Before you listen

Discuss the questions in a group.

1 What can we do differently now in these places thanks to technology?

at home   in the classroom   in the workplace

2 Which of these changes have you experienced personally?

C Global listening

🎧 **8.1** You will hear a discussion in a marketing company. Follow the stages, and identify what each person does.

Introduction

Chris starts the discussion.

1 Hailey **challenges / supports** the changes.

2 Chris **questions / justifies** the changes.

Topic 1

Chris introduces the topic of online communication.

3 Chris **outlines / questions** the advantages of online meetings.

4 Hailey **questions / agrees with** the effectiveness of technology.

5 Rashid **makes / asks for** a suggestion.

6 Chandini expresses **satisfaction with / concern about** the changes.

Topic 2

Chris introduces the topic of storing information.

7 Rashid **identifies / stops** a threat.

8 Chris **challenges / reassures** the group.

Topic 3

Chris introduces the topic of tablets.

9 Chandini **argues against / supports** the topic.

10 Chris **disagrees with / explains** the reasons for a decision.

D Close listening

> English is spoken by millions of people worldwide, sometimes as a first language and often as a learned second or third language. As users of English in today's world, we need to be prepared to deal with different accents and interact with different varieties of English.
>
> Gain exposure to different accents through listening to and watching programs from media channels around the world. As well as exposing you to different accents, this will also provide you with different perspectives on the world.
>
> When listening to different accents, practice identifying the key features of the accent. If you are going to a context where one accent is dominant, spend time familiarizing yourself with the accent before you arrive.
>
> Remember, varieties of English can also differ in the specific vocabulary used. Research differences and ask for clarification.

Following the way a discussion develops

Understanding non-standard accents

1 LISTENING

1 🎧 **8.1** Listen to the discussion again and decide if the sentences are *T* (True) or *F* (False).

1 Chris argues that though a system works now, it might not in the future. T / F

2 Hailey agrees that clients are no longer interested in face-to-face meetings. T / F

3 Chris suggests that recording meetings may be a negative action. T / F

4 Rashid mentions a colleague who would have worked effectively in this situation. T / F

5 Chandini explains the strength of her views on this issue. T / F

6 Rashid is concerned about competitors accessing confidential information. T / F

7 Chris explains that an outside company will be totally responsible for all levels of security. T / F

8 Hailey suggests that even top-level organizations face issues with security. T / F

9 Chandini knows about working on tablets from her domestic situation. T / F

10 Rashid agrees Chris's final point is a good idea. T / F

2 🎧 **8.2** Listen to each speaker from the discussion.

1 Which of the accents are more familiar to you?

2 Which are easier for you to understand? Why?

E Critical thinking

1 Work in pairs. Make a list of:

- the challenges of working with technology.
- the challenges of working without technology.

2 Share your lists with another pair. Do the lists change depending on the context (e.g., team members, location, task type)?

Study skills | Lecturers' varied approaches

Institutions have their own styles and rules. This is also true for different departments within an institution, and even for individual lecturers.

When you join a new institution or department, or when you begin a course with a new lecturer, spend time observing differences from your previous experience.

In lectures, consider:

- the lecture style.
- the amount of interaction expected.
- the type of support material provided.
- the amount of pre-reading and preparation expected.

For assignments, consider:

- the presentation and format.
- the mode of delivery.
- the amount of support provided.

© Stella Cottrell (2013)

1 Discuss the questions with a partner.

   1 What experiences have you had with different styles in a study context? Consider each point in the Study skills box.

   2 How did you change your approach in relation to the different styles?

   3 Would you do the same next time?

2 Read the extracts from two different lectures. Identify the parts that indicate the different styles of the lecturers.

> **Lecture 1**
> OK, so you'll need your handout from the tutorial. I assume you've all read it? You can see the outline of the lecture on this slide. We'll start with an overview of the main principle and where it came from. Then I'll focus the main part of the lecture on critical consequences resulting from it. At the end, there will be time for questions, so please keep your hands down until then. I've put a copy of the presentation on the shared drive. There's a reference to that on your handout, on page seven.

> **Lecture 2**
> What you are describing is the CNN effect. Can anyone explain what it is? Who's seen the news today? Everyone? Was it too complicated or could you follow it? Ed, did you get a little bit lost? Or did you focus on the sports? About the Feiler effect, could you explain it in one sentence, Amir?

3 Discuss the different lecturer styles with a partner.

   1 How would you describe each one?

   2 What are the positives and challenges of each style?

The changing pace of news

A Vocabulary preview

1 Match the words in the box with the correct definition.

1	**addictive** (adj)	a	all the things that need to be done, thought about, or solved
2	**agenda** (n)		
3	**angle** (n)	b	a particular way of thinking about something
4	**coverage** (n)	c	a chance to understand something or learn more about it
5	**exaggerate** (v)		
6	**insight** (n)	d	so enjoyable that you want to have it as often as possible
7	**perception** (n)	e	news about something on TV or radio or in the newspapers
8	**revert to** (v)		
		f	to return to a previous state or way of behaving
		g	a particular way of understanding or thinking about something
		h	to describe something in a way that makes it seem, e.g., better or worse than it really is

2 Complete the sentences with your views.

1 … is highly addictive and needs to be controlled.

2 … news coverage is the most reliable.

3 Companies tend to exaggerate …

4 In times of change, it is too easy to revert to …

5 … should make sure everyone is aware of the agenda.

6 People's perceptions are often …

7 We can get a great deal of insight by …

8 Broadcast companies need to find a particular angle to …

3 Compare your sentences from Exercise 2 with a partner. How many of each other's ideas do you agree with?

B Before you listen

Predicting lecture content

You are going to listen to a lecture about modern news coverage. First, work with a partner to make a list of the advantages and disadvantages of 24/7 news coverage.

C Global listening

1 🎧 8.3 Listen to part of a lecture. Which of your ideas from *Before you listen* are mentioned?

2 🎧 8.3 Listen to the part of the lecture again. Number the points in the order they are mentioned (1–7).

___ A news cycle involves the first report, followed by reaction to this.

___ Broadcasters compete to present news first.

___ Channels need audiences in order to make money from advertising.

_1_ Twenty-four-hour news provides continuous news coverage.

___ One broadcaster is concerned a fast pace of delivery has a negative effect.

___ The news cycle is much faster with 24/7 coverage.

___ The success of 24/7 coverage surprised many people.

3 🎧 8.4 Listen to part of another lecture. Number the questions in the order the lecturer asks them (1–4).

___ What you are describing is the CNN effect. Can anyone explain what it is?

___ So, what do you think will happen next?

___ For those of you who haven't read about the Feiler effect, could you explain it in one sentence?

___ What's the top news story today?

4 🎧 8.4 Listen again. Make notes on the answers given to each question. Then compare with a partner.

D Close listening

Understanding rapid, colloquial lecture speech

Some lecturers deliver their presentations in careful speech, designed to be understood by learners of English as well as native speakers. Other lecturers may use a faster, more colloquial speech, assuming the audience will understand.

… something will have to give … the top news story …
going to cover everything … the powers-that-be …

When speech is rapid and colloquial, listen for key words and concepts. These may be stressed and repeated.

Make a note of colloquial phrases. You may understand the individual words in these phrases but not be clear on the overall meaning. Check the meaning later.

Record the lecture and listen to it several times to build your understanding.

1 🎧 **8.5** Listen to eight extracts from the talk. Fill in the blanks with one or two words.

  1 Hi, guys! Sorry I'm _____ a little bit late …

  2 … but that's no excuse … so let's _____ and get started.

  3 … OK, we have a lot of _____ to do if we're going to cover everything we need to …

  4 … so _____ we last time? Did we get onto the CNN effect?

  5 I'm talking about the public perception that the powers-that-be are on _____, following _____, if you like.

  6 Because we have to be fast in a _____, twenty-four _____ world, right?

  7 That's a great point—you certainly know _____!

  8 It goes hand _____ with the CNN effect I'm talking about …

2 Discuss the meaning of each extract with a partner.

3 🎧 **8.6** Listen to two longer extracts from the second lecture. Write a short answer to each question.

Extract 1

  1 What does the lecturer apologize for at the start?

  2 What problem is there in relation to next week's lecture?

  3 Why does the lecturer refer to last week?

  4 What joke does the lecturer make about the student named Ed?

Extract 2

  5 How many different roles can the media have, according to the source quoted?

  6 What is the question connected to the second role?

  7 How does the public want to see their leaders?

  8 What kind of world do we live in nowadays, according to the lecturer?

E Critical thinking

Work in small groups. Discuss the questions.

1 What is the top news story today?

2 What do you think will happen next?

3 What will influence the development of the story positively? How?

4 What may influence the development of the story negatively? How?

Critical thinking

Personal incredulity

The fallacy of personal incredulity occurs when people find something difficult to understand. In this situation, people say that the thing they cannot understand must be untrue or not the case, because they personally are unable to understand it. The basic idea is as follows:

I cannot believe X or imagine how it could be true, therefore X must be false.

The fallacy can also work in the other direction.

I cannot believe X is false, so it must be true.

1   Read the extracts from the discussion. What does each person believe or not believe? What reason does the person give?

   1   Why change something that's working perfectly well for some system that's too complicated to even understand? Am I alone in thinking that this is just change for change's sake?

   2   You know as well as I do that clients want to meet face to face, to feel that someone actually cares about them! I don't believe they'll want to give that up. Online meetings just don't work.

   3   When I've been in online meetings, there are always technical problems—I can see the client, but they can't see me, that kind of thing. It just never works like it's supposed to!

   4   That's absolutely right, Rashid! How can we guarantee security if everything is going online? And I have all my files. I've spent the last two years improving my paper-based systems.

   5   I have my doubts. We read about security breaches at the highest government level almost every day … so, how are we going to protect ourselves? It will be impossible.

   6   How can we do our work on a tablet? They're good for simple tasks and some fun—I know, my children use one at home—but they simply aren't designed for sophisticated creative work!

2   How can the fallacy of personal incredulity be overcome? Make a list of things the person saying it, and also the person hearing it, could do.

Vocabulary development

Phrases for discussions

1 Complete the bold phrases in the sentences with the words in the box.

> ball finger guard outs record thoughts what words

1 It is not pleasant to **be lost for** _____, but everyone has experienced it at some time.

2 When you give a presentation, people expect you to **know** _____ **you're talking about**.

3 Don't quote what people tell you **off the** _____.

4 It is frustrating when you cannot **put your** _____ **on something**.

5 You are expected to **share your** _____ in a meeting, not only listen to others.

6 Often the most difficult part of a discussion is to **start the** _____ **rolling**.

7 We don't need to go into **the ins and** _____ of everything now. Let's talk generally.

8 People who don't like to **be caught off-**_____ in a discussion prepare well beforehand.

2 Match the phrases in bold in Exercise 1 with the definitions.

1 _____ tell someone what you are thinking

2 _____ all the details or facts that you need to know to deal with a situation

3 _____ be so surprised, shocked, etc., that you do not know what to say

4 _____ understand exactly why a situation is the way it is

5 _____ understand a subject very well, through experience of it

6 _____ surprised by something unexpected

7 _____ make something start happening

8 _____ used for saying that a remark is not official or public

3 Discuss the questions with a partner. **When was the last time you …**

- were lost for words?
- said something off the record?
- shared your thoughts on something?
- started the ball rolling in a discussion?

- didn't know what you were talking about?
- couldn't put your finger on the precise problem?
- discussed the ins and outs of something?
- were caught off-guard?

Academic words

1 Match the words in bold with the correct definitions.

1	**accumulation** (n)	a	the right or ability to make a judgment or decision
2	**compile** (v)	b	not easily changed
3	**discretion** (n)	c	the process by which something increases in amount
4	**enforce** (v)		
5	**persistent** (adj)	d	to keep something within strict limits
6	**mutual** (adj)	e	to make sure that a law or rule is obeyed by people
7	**restrict** (v)	f	felt or done in the same way by each of two or more people
8	**rigid** (adj)	g	continuing to do something in a determined way
		h	to make something by bringing together information from different places

2 Complete each sentence with a word in bold from Exercise 1.

1 The government should _____ tighter controls on news channels.

2 Broadcasting companies should _____ content more to protect children.

3 Definitions of "news" are too _____ in the era of social media.

4 You need to be _____ if you want to bring about major changes at work.

5 The _____ of online information will lead to problems for us all in the future.

6 To make big changes, you need to _____ evidence to show these changes are needed.

7 _____ is needed when posting online because what is private now could be public in the future.

8 Changes in news delivery have been of _____ benefit for those involved.

3 Choose the three sentences you most disagree with in Exercise 2. Change them so they match your views. Explain your choices to a partner.

Speaking model

You are going to learn about using past modals in conditionals when you speak, catenation and elision, and preparing and asking questions. You are then going to participate in a Q&A session about moving to a 100% digital classroom.

A Analyze

Read the discussion. Answer the questions.

1 What changes are being discussed?
2 Why does the college management want them?
3 Who is running the discussion: a lecturer, a member of the management team, or a student?

As you know, the college is proposing some major changes in the coming year. We're here today to discuss one of these—that is, changes to the courses offered by the college. The college has always offered the more traditional courses in language, business, and math. However, the thinking now is to move to more up-to-date, 21st-century courses. You've all read the information about these changes, so let's start the ball rolling … First question, please.

I have one—a fairly basic one … What exactly is the college planning to change?

Well, the idea is to offer courses that will appeal to employers and students alike. And remember, students are changing … you and I are already "old." To plan for future changes, we need to consider our younger brothers and sisters. What will they want to study? What jobs will they do in the future? The college has done that before. Just think, we would never have had our amazing technology courses if the college had focused on the present and the past. But we need to remember, change, by definition, never stops. These courses are already outdated.

So, can you give us some examples of specific courses the college wants to offer?

At this early stage, there is no list. The management wants to go through a period of consultation, with each party involved sharing their thoughts in an open and positive way. So these "parties" are obviously us, the students, but also the lecturers, the local employers, and even schools and, as I mentioned, the younger generation. However, the management doesn't want to restrict the discussion by always being involved. They learned that lesson from the discussions about changing college schedules. They acknowledge they shouldn't have tried to control the agenda. The whole process would have been a lot more positive if they had allowed student-centered discussion groups. But anyway … that's history now.

Why does the management think these changes are necessary now? Couldn't they wait until next year … the year after?

If education hadn't changed over the past few thousand years, we would still be counting with stones now. We have to move with the times. And those times are now.

When do you see the first of these courses being offered?

Well, off the record, I think it won't be until …

B Discuss

What would you change about the place where you study? How? Why? Share your ideas with a partner.

courses   facilities   schedules   technology use

Grammar

Past modals in conditionals

Past modals allow us to talk about past events that did not happen. We use the following structure:

If + had + past participle, would have + past participle
*If we **had planned** better, we **would have seen** improvements already.*

We can use *could* to show we think something would have happened, but we are not completely sure.

We use *should* and *shouldn't* to talk about things that were a good idea to do or not do, but the opposite happened.
*The management **should have told** us about the changes.*

Mixed conditionals

In mixed conditionals, the two clauses refer to different times.
*Fewer people **would be** unhappy now if they **had told** people about the changes.*
*If I had **wanted** to work with technology, I **would have chosen** a different career.*

1   🎧 8.7 Listen and complete the conditionals from Listening 1 and 2. What is the reality of each situation? Discuss the question with a partner.

   1 If we _____ about this last year, we _____ taken advantage of inviting Jackie …

   2 And sorry, Rashid, I _____ interrupted you, but I feel very strongly about this.

   3 I _____ bothered if I _____ we were going to get rid of all the paper and leave ourselves vulnerable online.

   4 If I _____ my laptop, I _____ been here on time.

2   Correct the grammar errors in the conditional sentences. Check your answers with the Speaking model.

   1 We would never have had our amazing technology courses if the college had focus on the present and the past.

   2 They acknowledge they shouldn't have try to control the agenda.

   3 The whole process would have been a lot more positive if they have allowed student-centered discussion groups.

   4 If education haven't changed over the past few thousand years, we would still be counting with stones now.

3   What is the reality of each situation in Exercise 2?

Speaking skill

When preparing questions for a Q&A session, consider asking questions from different angles.

Find out details

Who …?   What …?   Where …?   When …?   How …?

Elicit justifications

Why do you think …?   Why should …?

Ask for illustration of points made

Can you give an example of that?   What evidence is there for …?

Explore time frames

What do you see happening next year?

What has been the biggest lesson learned so far?

When did this trend begin?

Avoid loaded questions and questions that may be perceived as hostile. Make sure your interaction actually includes a question the speaker can answer. When you ask a question, consider your tone of voice, body language, and facial expression to ensure effective, open communication.

1   Review the Speaking model on page 146 and underline the questions asked. Identify the category of each question from the skills box.

2   🎧 8.8 Read and listen to the way the questions were asked from Listening 1. Identify the potential problems with each one.

> hostile   loaded   no question

1   … but anyway, what can we actually change? Do you have any concrete ideas?

2   … but isn't the technology a little bit clumsy?

3   … if I may ask a question. Sorry, Rashid … what you're saying is really worrying me. I don't see how we can be giving presentations about our campaigns online! It just isn't feasible, at all. I hear what you're saying, but I can't see how it will actually work in practice.

4   I'm completely lost for words. How can we do our work on a tablet?

3   Work in pairs to rewrite the extracts from Exercise 1 to make effective questions.

Pronunciation for speaking

Catenation and elision

Native speakers of English pronounce words in connected speech in the most efficient, fluent way. Precise pronunciation tends to be used by native speakers for specific purposes only, such as emphasizing a point. More usual natural pronunciation makes frequent use of linking (catenation) and leaving out sounds (elision).

Catenation

Speakers tend to link the final consonant sound of a word to the initial vowel sound of the next word. This can also happen when the first sound of the second word is a consonant that pairs naturally with the preceding consonant sound.

ask a question → *as ka question*   *as I said* → *a si said*

Elision

Vowel sounds from unstressed syllables are often elided in natural connected speech. Consonant sounds /t/ and /d/ are often left out, particularly when in groups of consonants. The /h/ sound is also often omitted.

not that → *no(t) that*   *and not just here* → *'n(d) no(t) just here*

I have been → *I've been*

1 🎧 8.9 Listen to and read the extracts. Identify one or two examples of catenation or elision in each.

   1 You've all read the directive?
   2 So, the first one is communication.
   3 And not just here, but also meeting clients online.
   4 … it'll be a big time saver for everyone.
   5 … we'll need proper training and support.
   6 … if I may ask a question.

2 🎧 8.10 Review the extracts. Predict where catenation or elision will occur. Then listen and check.

   1 Can I move on to the next thing?
   2 You don't sound negative at all.
   3 … what works now isn't going to work in five, ten, 15 years, right?
   4 It's just a question of deciding what needs to be done face to face.
   5 We're going to be a paperless office, as far as possible.
   6 I can tell you that we'll be getting a very secure system.

3 Work with a partner. Practice saying the extracts from Exercises 1 and 2.

Speaking task

Take part in a Q&A session about moving to a 100% digital classroom.

Brainstorm

Review *All change, please* and *The changing pace of news* and the Speaking lesson.

- Identify the challenges and benefits of using technology in education.
- Identify the challenges and benefits of changing an educational context.
- Research facts and statistics related to digital classrooms.

Plan

Review and organize your ideas and research. What questions does your material answer?

Prepare a brief presentation outlining a plan to move to a 100% digital classroom. In addition, prepare a set of eight questions about moving to a 100% digital classroom.

Speak

Get together with another pair. Have a Q&A session. One pair asks questions, the other pair answers.

Share

Discuss the experience of taking part in a Q&A. What were the challenges? What were the rewards?

Work with a new pair. Change roles to experience the other side of a Q&A session.

Reflect

Using the information you learned throughout the unit, answer the questions.

1 What are the benefits of asking questions?
2 What strategies can people use to cope with change?
3 Which is more important, stability and continuity, or development and change?

Review

Wordlist

Vocabulary preview

addictive (adj)	directive (n) **	insight (n) **
agenda (n) **	do away with (v)	perception (n) **
angle (n) ***	exaggerate (v) *	revert to (v) *
campaign (n) ***	feasible (adj) *	vulnerable (adj) **
coverage (n) **	glimpse (n) *	
cutthroat (adj)	infrastructure (n) *	

Vocabulary development

be caught off-guard	off the record	start the ball rolling
be lost for words	put your finger on something	the ins and outs
know what you're talking about	share your thoughts	

Academic words

accumulation (n)	enforce (v) **	restrict (v) **
compile (v) **	mutual (adj) **	rigid (adj) **
discretion (n) **	persistent (adj) **	

Academic words review

Complete the sentences with the correct form of the words in the box.

accumulation	equivalent	mutual	policy	restrict

1 Janelle admires Dr. Smith's work, and the respect is _____.
2 It is college _____ to prosecute plagiarism. You should have known that.
3 There is nothing we can do to _____ the movement of the invasive species.
4 The _____ of space garbage in the orbit is a serious problem – each year, there is more risk of collision.
5 A full bus can take the _____ of 20 car passengers off the road.

Unit review

Listening 1	☐	I can understand non-standard accents.
Listening 2	☐	I can understand rapid, colloquial speech.
Study skill	☐	I can deal with lecturers' varied approaches.
Vocabulary	☐	I can use phrases to describe discussions.
Grammar	☐	I can use past modals in conditionals.
Speaking	☐	I can prepare and ask questions for discussions.

Discussion point

Study the infographic about oceans, and answer the questions.

1 Which of the categories is most important in your region of the world?

2 What negative effects might some of the points have on the world's oceans?

3 How should we prioritize the uses of the ocean?

4 What are the most important future considerations for the ocean?

Why are oceans important?

Food

- Fish is the main source of protein for **1 billion** people in developing countries.

Economy

- **76%** of U.S. trade involves marine transportation.
- Ecotourism connected to the reefs makes **$9 billion** annually.
- International trade in fish and fish products globally is **$102 billion** per year.

Jobs

- Of all the people globally earning their living from fishing, **90%** live in developing countries.
- **350 million** jobs worldwide linked to oceans.

Climate

- Five times more carbon is stored by habitats close to the ocean than by tropical forests.
- The ocean produces more than **50%** of the world's oxygen.

VIDEO

SUN, SEA, AND ENERGY

Before you watch

Match the words in bold with the correct definitions.

1 **combat** (v)
2 **leg** (n)
3 **panel** (n)
4 **promote** (v)
5 **renewable** (adj)

a a flat object that is attached to a surface

b describing an energy that can replace itself by natural processes

c to encourage the use of something

d to fight against / prevent

e part of a journey

UNIT AIMS

LISTENING 1 Listening to interpret idioms
LISTENING 2 Making estimates and hypotheses
STUDY SKILL How effective am I in giving presentations and talks?

VOCABULARY Phrases for describing conditions
GRAMMAR Complex ordering of past events
SPEAKING Transitions in presentations

A scuba-diver's encounter with a whale.

While you watch

Watch the video and choose *T* (True) or *F* (False).

1 The Greenpeace ship is solar powered. T / F
2 Greenpeace is an international organization. T / F
3 There are regular power cuts in Lebanon. T / F
4 Using solar energy is better for people's health. T / F
5 Solar panels are much cheaper in Lebanon because more people use them. T / F

After you watch

Discuss these questions in a group.

1 What kind of energy sources are most common in your country?
2 What kinds of renewable energy would be suitable for your country? Why?
3 What do you think could be done to raise people's awareness of renewable energy sources?
4 What do you think are the biggest obstacles to the use of renewable energy sources?

The history of surfing

A Vocabulary preview

1 Read the sentences. Match the words in bold with the correct definitions below.

1 Being **youthful** is a question of attitude rather than age.
2 One day humans will be able to **tame** nature.
3 Social media can easily be used to **popularize** a product.
4 Scientists need to show **caution** when they interfere with nature.
5 The best thing about small vehicles is that they are easier to **maneuver**.
6 People tend to **associate** water with danger.
7 Some natural **fibers** are stronger than human-made fibers.
8 Different languages use different **metaphors** to describe nature.

a _____ (n) a long, thin piece of a natural or artificial substance, similar to a thread or hair in shape

b _____ (n) a word or phrase used to refer to something different in order to emphasize the two things' similar qualities

c _____ (v) to perform an action or movement that you need care or skill to do

d _____ (v) to bring something under control

e _____ (v) to form a connection in your mind between different people or things

f _____ (v) to make something popular with many people

g _____ (n) careful thought and lack of hurry in order to try to avoid risks or danger

h _____ (adj) typical of young people

2 Which of the sentences do you agree with in Exercise 1? Compare your answers with a partner.

B Before you listen

Work with a partner. You are going to listen to a program about surfing. What aspects of the sport might each person interviewed in the program talk about?

An academic author

A professional surfer

A music and culture critic

C Global listening

🎧 **9.1** Listen to a program about surfing. Match the sentence parts to complete a summary of the program.

1 The host introduces   a how she became interested in the sport.
2 The writer identifies   b an error of thought.
3 The writer outlines   c the history of surfing.
4 The host introduces   d a surfer.
5 The surfer describes   e a writer.
6 The surfer explains   f specific benefits of being a surfer.
7 The surfer identifies   g how surfers feel about the sport.
8 The surfer describes   h a theory about the popularization of surfing.
9 The host introduces   i a critic.
10 The critic provides   j features of the equipment used.

D Close listening

> Idioms are fixed expressions that use images and metaphor to describe things.
>
> *They must have had **nerves of steel**, given the size of the waves and the design of the boards, which were actually made to be difficult to maneuver.*
>
> Idioms can be difficult for language learners because the connections between image and idea may not be immediately obvious. Idioms in the learner's own language may use different ideas and images. However, despite these differences, it is often possible to deduce the meaning of the expression.
>
> - Think about the context the idiom was used in.
> - Consider the actual meaning of words in the idiom.
> - Look for connections and relationships with the context.

1 🎧 **9.2** Listen to extracts from the interviews and complete the idioms.

1 **Dicing with** _____ was an important part of the activity.

2 The town _____ **to bursting** with surfers from all over the world.

3 I loved to watch them and I suppose that's when the **bug** _____.

4 … only **a** _____ of surfers ever **strike it** _____.

5 … but we **don't** _____ **over spilled** _____.

6 They can _____ **an arm and a leg** for professionals.

7 … using artificial materials was a **quantum** _____ in surfboard construction.

8 To be honest, **your** _____ **is as good as mine**! Part of it is just the **luck of the** _____.

2 🎧 **9.3** Listen to parts of the program again and choose the correct answers.

1 What was one of the key points of surfing in ancient times in Tahiti?
   a to show you were prepared to take part in a dangerous activity
   b to show you were as brave as the rulers of the community

2 Which statement describes Jen's experience of getting involved in surfing?
   a She was surrounded by surfers where she lived and this helped her develop an interest.
   b She knew a lot of surfers, but she didn't get interested until later in her life.

3 According to Jen, in what way is surfing different from sports such as tennis and golf?
   a It is not possible to do it as a full-time job.
   b Hardly any participants make a lot of money from the sport.

4 What attitude do surfers tend to have about difficulties, according to Jen?
   a They are not worried by challenges and failure.
   b They spend a lot of time thinking about what went wrong.

5 What can be said about professional surfboards?
   a They are covered in fiberglass cloth and are good for surfing.
   b They are made of hi-tech material and are extremely expensive.

6 What is Jen's response when asked if she is going to win?
   a There is no way of predicting.
   b The host would have a better chance.

E Critical thinking

Work in groups. Read the quotes from the interviews and discuss the related questions. Share your views with another group.

It's a strange sport, in a way, because the more adverse the conditions, like today, the happier we are!

1 Why do some people choose to participate in dangerous activities?

But, you know, a lot of people, even surfers, have some strange ideas about where surfing came from.

2 How much do the origins of an activity matter to people doing them now?

Study skills   How effective am I in giving presentations and talks?

We have different strengths as speakers. It is useful to reflect on these skills and also to identify areas we could improve. However, to be most effective, as well as identifying areas for improvement, we also need to make a plan for how to improve.

Use a checklist to identify your strengths and areas for improvement. For example:

Aspect of giving a talk	Rating	How could I improve this aspect?
1 Was my main argument clear?	1 2 3 4 5	*Clearly identify the main point when planning the presentation and make sure I signpost this to the audience and include enough examples and supporting points.*

1 Read the checklist and rate how effective you are in each aspect of giving a talk. Make notes on how to improve in each aspect.

Aspects of giving a talk	Rating	How could I improve this aspect?
1 How good was my opening?	1 2 3 4 5	
2 Did I begin with a brief outline?	1 2 3 4 5	
3 Did I stick to my outline?	1 2 3 4 5	
4 Was my main argument clear?	1 2 3 4 5	
5 Did I sum up at the end?	1 2 3 4 5	
6 How well did I finish?	1 2 3 4 5	
7 How appropriate were my handouts or audiovisual aids?	1 2 3 4 5	

© Stella Cottrell (2013)

2 Compare your ratings and notes with a partner. Discuss other ways to improve and add to your notes.

3 What other aspects of a presentation can be worked on? Consider the ideas in the box. Then compare your list with a partner. Then work together to prepare a checklist with a question for each aspect you identified.

> audience   different viewpoints   examples   eye contact and body language
> feedback   order of points   questions

4 Exchange checklists with another pair. Use the new checklist to review your strengths in other aspects of presentation giving. Identify ways to improve.

Ocean problems

A Vocabulary preview

1 Match the words in bold with the correct definitions.

1	**alarming** (adj)	a	describing a place or society with a lot of industry
2	**consumption** (n)	b	an amount of something that is produced or gathered
3	**hypothesis** (n)	c	an idea that attempts to explain something, but has not yet been tested or proved
4	**industrialized** (adj)	d	frightening or worrying
5	**overestimate** (v)	e	a refusal to accept something new such as a plan, idea, or change
6	**reproduce** (v)	f	the process of buying or using goods
7	**resistance** (n)	g	to make a mistake by providing an amount or number that is too high
8	**yield** (n)	h	to repeat or produce something in the same way as before

2 Complete the sentences using your own ideas.

1 It can be alarming when …

2 An example of a famous hypothesis is …

3 Industrialized countries should be responsible for …

4 An example of an experiment that's difficult to reproduce is …

5 In farming, the yield can be increased by …

6 Nowadays, in many places, there is more resistance to …

7 People tend to overestimate …

8 Our consumption of products needs to …

3 Compare your sentences from Exercise 2 with a partner. How many of each other's ideas do you agree with?

B Before you listen

You are going to listen to part of a lecture covering two specific problems faced by the world's oceans.

1 Make a list of the possible problems you are aware of.

2 Work in pairs. Share your lists and discuss potential solutions.

C Global listening

1 🎧 9.4 Listen to the introduction to the lecture. Does the lecturer discuss problems from your list?

2 🎧 9.5 Predict how to complete the outline for the lecture using the words from the box. Listen and check.

Listening to complex arguments

> causes   community   efficiency   examples   figures
> phenomenon   predators   reproduce   small   solutions

Marine ecology—problems and solutions

A Overfishing

1   *Three types*

   i.   *"recruitment overfishing"—amount of fish taken > than amount possible to* ¹ __predator__ ~~reproduce~~ *→ fish population decreases*

   ii.   *"growth overfishing"—fish too* ² __small__ *to produce the best yield are taken*

   iii.   *"ecosystem overfishing"—damages balance of ecosystem, e.g.,* ³ __predators__ *are overfished, leaving too many small fish*

2   ⁴ __figures__ *supporting seriousness of problem*

   i.   *size of illegal catch*

   ii.   *decrease in number of species*

3   *Example of* ⁵ __community__ *affected by overfishing in Canada: history → problem → effect → solution*

4   ⁶*Human* __figures__ ~~efficiency~~ *: problem → regulation → resistance*

5   *Other possible* ⁷ __solutions__ *:*

   i.   *aquaculture*

   ii.   *raising consumer awareness*

B Coral bleaching

1   ⁸ __phenomenon__ *—coral loses color*

2   ⁹ __causes__

   i.   *change of conditions*

   ii.   *human influence*

3   ¹⁰ __examples__ *of coral bleaching—U.S., Maldives, and Sri Lanka*

Making estimates and hypotheses

D Close listening

> **Hypotheses**
>
> Speakers often present facts and statistics about a situation, and then make a hypothesis to provide a possible explanation for this situation. The more supporting information and/or agreement among experts, often the stronger the hypothesis.
>
> **Estimates**
>
> Exact research statistics may not always be available or result from research studies. However, it is often possible to make an estimate based on information presented. Speakers may present estimates from experts, or estimates they make themselves.

1 🎧 **9.6** Listen to extracts from the talk. Match the extracts with the hypotheses presented.

1 _____
2 _____
3 _____
4 _____

a Most people focus on the cost rather than the source when purchasing food.

b People are responsible for how fragile the coral reefs are.

c Regulation will not be effective when employment and income are affected.

d Oceans have been harmed by three different types of overfishing.

2 🎧 **9.7** Listen to the extracts and complete the details for the estimates.

I Estimated amount of illegal fish caught per year [1] ____11 - 26 million____ tons, representing [2] ___24 - 32 %___ of the annual global catch

II Decrease in marine species in the past four decades estimated at [3] ___Fourel 40%___, with [4] ___1/3rd___ of fish stocks overfished

III 1992 cod population estimated to be [5] ___1 %___ of previous amount and an estimated [6] ___35,0000___ jobs lost

IV 2015 cod stocks up to around [7] ___2/3___ of original amount (but this figure is seen by some as an overestimation)

V Estimated amount of Caribbean coral reef lost by the U.S. in 2005— [8] ___50 %___; estimates of coral bleaching in parts of the Indian Ocean in 2016—[9] ___90%___.

E Critical thinking

Discuss the questions in a group.

Why is it important to develop hypotheses? How can hypotheses be tested?

What should researchers do with the findings of their studies?

Critical thinking

Appeal to nature

An argument that suggests something is good because it is "natural" is an appeal to nature.

Fishing is a natural way for humans to get food. Therefore, it cannot be seen as a problem.

The issue with this type of argument arises from the assumption that everything natural is good. This assumption can be seen as either meaningless or a matter of opinion; it is not the basis of a logical argument. The word *natural* can also be a loaded word, and associated with words such as *normal*. This association has a value judgment —*normal* is right, good, correct.

The opposite form of the argument is also used, i.e., if something is not natural, it is bad.

Controlling the type of fish caught is not a natural process, so it shouldn't be done.

1   Discuss the extracts from the interviews and the lecture with a partner. Identify the appeals to nature.

   1   But aren't surfboards that are made of wood better? They're more natural, and that's how people have always done it, according to Oliwa, right?

   2   My family worries sometimes, and one of my friends says I'm crazy to take the risks I do. But I say it feels so natural for us surfers to do it—so it would be wrong not to do it … right?

   3   They popularized the surfing sound in the early 1960s, where surfing served as a metaphor, if you like, for a youthful, healthy, cool, post-war younger generation … getting back in touch with nature, rejecting their parents' values …

   4   The … coral rejects the algae that it contains and on which it depends for approximately 90% of its energy. Again, there are those who will say that it's a natural phenomenon, that change is a part of nature, and therefore we shouldn't worry about it …

2   🎧 9.8 Listen to the extracts. Identify the appeals to nature and the counter arguments presented.

3   Discuss the questions in a group.

   1   What common appeals to nature are you aware of in the following areas?

         food   medicine   raising children   travel

   2   What are some counter arguments?

Vocabulary development

Words for describing conditions

1 Match the words from the box with the correct meaning.

> adverse conditions   bleak   comparative safety   devastation
> fragile   thriving   unspoiled   viable

1 _____ (adj) not changed in ways that make it less beautiful or enjoyable

2 _____ (adj) easy to break or damage

3 _____ (phrase) circumstances that make it difficult or unpleasant for something to happen or exist

4 _____ (adj) very successful

5 _____ (adj) without any reasons to feel happy or hopeful

6 _____ (phrase) a situation judged to be safe in comparison to something else

7 _____ (adj) able to live and grow in an independent way

8 _____ (n) damage or destruction affecting a large area or a lot of people

2 Describe the following places you know to your partner.

1 somewhere that is **bleak**

2 an **unspoiled** environment

3 a place of **comparative safety**

4 somewhere that has seen a lot of **devastation**

5 a city that is **thriving**

6 a **fragile** environment

7 somewhere that is **viable** to live without transportation

8 a place that has **adverse conditions** for human life

Academic words

1 Match the words in bold with the correct definitions.

1	**convention** (n)	a	very small or insignificant
2	**dimension** (n)	b	to provide the conditions in which something can happen or exist
3	**domain** (n)		
4	**duration** (n)	c	the period of time during which something continues to happen
5	**marginal** (adj)		
6	**rely on** (v)	d	to trust someone or something to do something for you
7	**sustain** (v)	e	length, height, or width
8	**underlie** (v)	f	to be the real or basic cause of or reason for something
		g	a particular area or activity of life
		h	a way of behaving that is generally accepted as being normal and right

2 Complete each sentence with a word in bold from Exercise 1.

1 We shouldn't ask experts for their opinion outside of their professional _____.

2 We cannot _____ governments to protect the environment.

3 We tend not to worry about things beyond the _____ of our lifetime.

4 The gains made from individual efforts to recycle are _____.

5 The _____ of a room are more important than the light in it.

6 To _____ our way of life, we all need to make changes.

7 Most people naturally want to follow _____.

8 To understand a problem such as overfishing, we need to look at the issues that _____ it.

3 Choose the three sentences you most agree or disagree with in Exercise 2. Explain your choices to a partner.

Speaking model

You are going to learn about describing complex ordering of past events when you speak, using intonation to attract and keep interest, and transitions in presentations. You are then going to deliver a presentation on ways to use water more effectively.

A Analyze

Read the extract from a presentation. Answer the questions.

1 What is the general topic of the presentation?
2 What specific area does the speaker focus on in this section?
3 Identify any estimations included.

Many of us take the endless supply of hot water streaming from our taps for granted. However, we don't need to go back far into the past to realize how privileged we are. The 19th century saw the invention of the first domestic water heater, making hot water more easily accessible. However, it was still only those with money who benefited, though not safely, I might add, due to the dangerous construction of these early heaters. Before that, there had been various systems for heating water in use since Roman times, but each of those had their downside. Let's take a look at some of those now, starting with the Romans.

This image shows how the Romans built settlements around natural sources of hot water, channeling this heated water into bathhouses. This system worked to an extent. However, while the rich and powerful were busy making use of this natural source, the more disadvantaged in society remained without hot water.

Moving to the post-Roman era, the practice of burning fuel to heat water over fires was used for centuries throughout all levels of society. However, these fires were often in houses with poor ventilation, making the getting of hot water both dirty and dangerous.

It is this next invention that we have to thank for our seemingly endless supplies of hot water: the modern domestic gas or electric water heater, bringing hot water to many of us with the simple flick of a switch. However, as we shall see, this ease of access brings with it several environmental issues. Let's take a look at some numbers.

In the U.K., it is estimated that 10% of the total amount of water use is in the domestic domain. Though this is small in comparison to the 70% for agriculture and 20% for industry, it is by no means insignificant. And it's not just the actual amount of water use that is an issue, as we can see here.

It is estimated that as much as 25% of the domestic energy bill in the U.K. is from heating water. However, our wonderful water heaters result in a heavy usage of energy. And since this energy is not environmentally friendly, hot water is a burden on the environment. In the U.K., water heaters account for 5% of U.K. greenhouse gas emissions.

So, what can individuals do to help alleviate these issues?

B Discuss

Discuss the questions in a group. Explain and support your views.

1 In what ways do you try to reduce your water consumption?
2 How can people be encouraged to reduce their water consumption further?

Grammar

Complex ordering of past events

In higher-level texts, the description of an event or period of time may not follow the chronological order. The description may move backwards and forwards in time, and often requires precise use of a combination of tenses and linkers.

*The activity certainly **predates** that first glimpse foreigners **had** of it— Tahitians **had been surfing** for centuries. It **had been** a part of ancient Polynesian culture.*

Simultaneous events and interruptions may also be included.

*Anyway, in Cornwall, **whenever** I could, I'd borrow a board and have a go. **At about that time** I heard about Margo Oberg.*

1   Annotate the timeline with the list of events and periods of time in the box.

Some form of surfing has probably been practiced for as long as humans have been swimming, but the modern art of surfing was first seen by Joseph Banks on board the HMS *Endeavour* in the 18th century, when the ship stopped in Tahiti in the Polynesian islands. That seems to be the birthplace, and the activity certainly predates that first glimpse foreigners had of it—Tahitians had been surfing for centuries. It had been a part of ancient Polynesian culture.

  a Humans begin swimming   b Some form of surfing is practiced
  c Banks's ship stops in Tahiti   d Joseph Banks sees the modern art of surfing
  e Surfing is part of Tahitian culture

2    9.9 Complete the extract from Listening 1 with the verb in parentheses in an appropriate tense. Listen and check. (More than one answer may be correct.)

It really [1] _____ (start) when my family [2] _____ (move) to Cornwall in England, a surfer's paradise. Before that, I [3] _____ (live) in a seaside town in Portugal, where there [4] _____ (be) some good waves. Every summer, the town filled to bursting with surfers from all over the world: Australians, Swiss, everyone [5] _____ (come) to ride the waves. I loved to watch them and I suppose that's when the bug bit. Anyway, in Cornwall, whenever I [6] _____ (can), I [7] _____ (borrow) a board and have a go. At about that time I heard about Margo Oberg, who really inspired me—she became the first female professional surfer in the same year that professional contests started, 1975. And I think before that I [8] _____ (read) an article about the first superstar surfer, Kelly Slater, which kind of caught my attention … I [9] _____ (get) my first sponsor when I was 16, and since then I [10] _____ (spend) all my time chasing the waves all over the world.

past

1 —

2 —

3 —

4 —

5 —

present

Speaking skill

Help the audience to follow your ideas and ensure that you stay on track with your plan by using transitions between main points. As you move from one visual to another, transitions linking the sections help the listeners engage and also anticipate the upcoming material. Good speakers signpost what they will talk about, sometimes using questions to engage the audience *before* moving to the next slide, to alert the audience to what they are about to see.

… often catastrophically in both cases. **Let me give you an example on this next slide.** *As you can see, it concerns …*

… the majority of studies show. **However, as we will see,** *things have changed. This chart shows …*

… concerning this issue. **But what did the studies reveal? Well, as the chart clearly shows** *…*

1   Review the transitions from the lecture. Underline the phrases and questions used.

1   Together, these three are thought to be the culprits in the damage done to our ocean ecosystems. So, just how serious is this problem? Well, this next slide has some alarming figures.

2   Coastal communities that depend on fish are affected, as is the balance of ocean life, often catastrophically in both cases. Let me give you an example, on this next slide. As you can see, it concerns the eastern Canadian cod-fishing industry off Newfoundland and Labrador.

3   But now, thankfully, the cod are viable again. Which moves us on to solutions. What was the solution in this case? Simple: a complete ban for an initial duration of two years—later extended—on cod fishing in the area.

2   🎧 9.10 Listen and complete the transition phrases and questions. Mark the most effective place to change to the next visual.

1   But there's always likely to be resistance against regulatory measures from a fishing industry that feels that its workers' livelihoods are threatened. So, _____? Well, one is aquaculture, or farming fish in captivity.

2   Therefore, though a great initiative, it is unlikely to solve the problem in the long term. So, that's enough input on overfishing for now. _____ the phenomenon known as "coral bleaching."

3   One hypothesis is that the sunscreen may harm the reefs just as much as increased temperature. So, now, _____, as marine ecological engineers, how can we address …

3   Review the model and underline the phrases and questions the speaker uses to transition between slides.

Pronunciation for speaking

Using intonation to attract and keep interest

Appropriate, engaging intonation is important for attracting and maintaining the listeners' interest.

Good speakers divide their speech into chunks with one main stressed syllable and the main intonation movement starting on this syllable. They also vary their pitch, moving between a highest and lowest point. (How high and low these points are depends on the speaker.)

When giving a presentation, to keep your audience engaged and listening, avoid flat intonation with little or no pitch change. Identify the pauses, main stresses, and intonation movements in your script. Then practice the presentation. Get feedback on the level of engagement and work on any areas that need improvement.

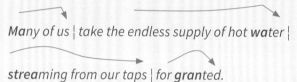

*Many of us ¦ take the endless supply of hot **water** ¦*

*strea**ming** from our taps ¦ for **granted.***

1   🔊 9.11 Listen and read the extracts with the pauses marked. Identify the pitch changes with arrows.

   1   In many countries today, | fresh water is not a given | – but a luxury.
   2   It's easy to believe this: | as long as we have water, | there is no need to worry.
   3   However | – even water in our taps, | which we consider healthy, | concerns many scientists.
   4   If we are to ensure | safe access to water, | there are several steps | which most communities can take today.

2   Practice the extracts. Follow the pauses and pitch changes to make the intonation engaging.

3   Work in pairs. Review the next part of the Speaking model. Then mark the pauses and pitch changes. Practice delivering parts of the model in an engaging, interesting way.

Speaking task

Give a presentation on ways to use water more effectively.

Brainstorm

Review *The history of surfing* and *Ocean problems* and the Speaking lesson. Then work in pairs to do the following.

- Choose an area of water use: private, company, or public.
- Identify ways water is used in the chosen area.
- Identify ways water could be used more efficiently.

Research facts and statistics related to each of the areas you identify. Also, find out about a historic aspect of the area of water use.

Plan

With your partner, review and organize your notes. Select the three most significant ways to use water more efficiently in your chosen area.

Then plan your presentation. Include an explanation of a historic aspect of the subject. Plan to use visuals and transitions between the main points. Practice delivering the presentation in an engaging way.

Speak

Work in a new group. Take turns giving your presentations. Ask questions at the end of the other students' presentations.

Share

Discuss your presentations as a group. Comment on the transitions and how effective they were. Then work with your first partner again. Compare your experiences with giving the presentation. Do you agree on which parts were most effective?

Reflect

Using the information you learned throughout the unit, answer the questions.

1 What are some of the key roles water plays in our lives?
2 What other areas of nature do we need to protect? Why? How?
3 What are the greatest improvements you have made in delivering presentations?

Review

Wordlist

MACMILLAN
DICTIONARY

Vocabulary preview

alarming (adj)	industrialized (adj)	resistance (n) ***
associate (v) ***	maneuver (v) *	tame (v)
caution (n) **	metaphors (n) *	yield (n) *
consumption (n) **	overestimate (v)	youthful (adj)
fibers (n)	popularize (v)	
hypothesis (n) *	reproduce (v) **	

Vocabulary development

adverse conditions (n)	devastation (n)	unspoiled (adj)
bleak (adj) *	fragile (adj) *	viable (adj) *
comparative safety (n)	thriving (adj)	

Academic words

convention (n) ***	duration (n) **	sustain (v) **
dimension (n) **	marginal (adj) *	underlie (v)
domain (n) **	rely on (v) ***	

Academic words review

Complete the sentences with the correct form of the words in the box.

convention	domain	enforce	guidelines	ignorance

1 If you had followed the _____, there would be no trouble.
2 The rules had always been there—but this year, the institute began to _____ them in earnest.
3 Most people can claim _____ when it comes to damaging the oceans—but not sailors!
4 Hundreds of people attended the _____ on sustainable fishing.
5 Sven's thinking skills are of no use to him in the interpersonal _____.

Unit review

Listening 1		I can listen to interpret idioms.
Listening 2		I can make estimates and hypotheses while listening.
Study skill		I can evaluate the effectiveness of my presentations.
Vocabulary		I can use phrases for describing conditions.
Grammar		I can use structures for complex ordering of past events.
Speaking		I can use transitions in presentations.

10 CONFLICT

Conflict in the courts

Discussion point

Study the infographic about courts and compensation, and discuss the questions.

1 Which of these cases is valid in your opinion? Which would you dismiss?

2 Why do some people actively seek conflict, e.g., in the law courts?

3 To what extent is conflict inevitable in life?

4 Would the world be perfect if there was no conflict?

£7,000 compensation sought for a physical attack by a bird

The injured woman wanted the owners of her office building, on top of which the bird lived, to pay up… Case dismissed.

£8,000 or a full-size car wanted

After winning a car in a competition, a woman was devastated to find out it was a toy car. She sued the company for the price of the full-size car. Success.

Misrepresentation of orca whales

The family of a man killed after illegally swimming with whales sued the theme park for failing to advertise the fact that whales can kill. Case dropped.

$12,000 awarded for tooth loss

A woman was awarded the money plus all dental expenses after losing two front teeth when falling through a window into a club. The unusual entry was to avoid the $3.50 entry fee.

VIDEO

SMASH THINGS, FEEL BETTER

Before you watch

Match the words in bold with the correct definitions.

1 **bash** (v)   a   impressive
2 **hard-hatted** (adj)   b   to damage
3 **mindless** (adj)   c   to destroy
4 **slick** (adj)   d   to give expression to strong emotions
5 **trash** (v)   e   to hit
6 **vent** (v)   f   wearing a protective helmet
7 **wreak destruction** (phrase)   g   without thought for consequences

UNIT AIMS

LISTENING 1 Anticipating information to come
LISTENING 2 Coping with different lecture styles
STUDY SKILL Where next?

VOCABULARY Words for describing behavior
GRAMMAR Using adverbs to modify statements
SPEAKING Principles and structure of formal debates

Two soccer players exchanging frank opinions.

While you watch

Choose the correct option to complete the sentences.

1 The destruction of the hotel was **a psychology experiment / a publicity event / accidental**.

2 The people selected to take part were chosen because **they had stressful jobs / they passed a psychological test / they were stressed**.

3 After destroying the hotel rooms, the participants felt **guilty / happy / more violent**.

4 The hotel was used for this because **it is being renovated / it is being sold / it is being demolished**.

After you watch

Tell others in your group about…

1 a time you felt particularly stressed.

2 something you intentionally destroyed or damaged.

3 what you do to reduce your stress levels.

4 a time you accidentally broke something of value.

5 whether you would like to take part in destroying the hotel.

Conflict resolution—what works best?

A Vocabulary preview

1 Match the words in bold with the correct definitions.

1	**conciliation** (n)	a	certainly correct or true
2	**empathy** (n)	b	based on theories or ideas instead of on practical experience
3	**fake** (adj)	c	made to look like something real in order to trick people
4	**preventative** (adj)	d	a process that is intended to end an argument between two groups of people
5	**proposition** (n)	e	done so that something does not become worse or turn into a problem
6	**resolution** (n)	f	the action of solving a problem or dealing with a disagreement in a satisfactory way
7	**theoretical** (adj)	g	the ability to understand how someone feels because you can imagine what it is like to be them
8	**undeniable** (adj)	h	a statement that people can examine in order to decide whether it is true

2 Complete the sentences with the words in the boxes. Change the form if necessary.

> empathy   fake   resolutions   theoretical

1 Real-life experience must always be supported by _____ arguments.

2 The most effective _____ are agreed to by everyone involved.

3 Without _____, agreement cannot be reached.

4 All sources of information should be carefully checked to ensure it is not _____.

> conciliation   preventative   proposition   undeniable

5 _____ is always easier when a third, neutral party is involved.

6 It is _____ that conflict causes stress.

7 A _____ needs careful examination before being accepted.

8 _____ measures are usually cheaper than finding solutions for a problem.

3 Which of the sentences do you agree with? Compare your answers with a partner.

B Before you listen

You will hear a debate about proactive and yielding methods of dealing with conflict. Discuss the questions with a partner.

1 What methods do people use to deal with conflict? Make a list.

2 Which methods confront conflict and which attempt to prevent it?

C Global listening

Listening to confirm predictions

1 Read the list of methods for managing conflict. Predict which may be suggested by a proactive style, and which by a yielding style. Choose *P* (Proactive) or *Y* (Yielding).

___ Offer positive reasons for the other side to change their position P / Y

___ Make the effort to understand your opponents' viewpoint P / Y

_1_ Cooperate with your opponents by doing some, but not all, of what they want P / Y

___ Do what the other side wants you to do in order to maintain a good relationship P / Y

___ Avoid situations in which the stronger side is able to dominate P / Y

___ Do nothing and wait for the situation to resolve itself P / Y

2 🎧 10.1 Listen to a debate about dealing with conflict. Number the techniques in Exercise 1 in the order you hear them (1–6). Were your predictions correct?

D Close listening

Anticipating information to come

> Skillful listeners use all the available information to predict information the speaker will give. Anticipating in this way supports the listeners: as the speaker continues, the listeners confirm their predictions and/or identify new themes in the communication.
>
> • Read through the information available about the lecture or discussion, e.g., handouts, notes, etc.
>
> • Review titles and visuals and consider their connection to the topic.
>
> • Anticipate missing information, e.g.:
>   • What kind of information is missing?
>   • What has the speaker not discussed yet?
>   • What stage of the argument is missing?
>
> • Predict other topics or themes the speaker may cover.

1 Review the outline of the debate with a partner. Discuss and predict the missing details and arguments.

Proactive conflict management	Yielding conflict management
Speaker 1	
Cooperative methods are 1 _____	**Speaker 2**
Results are 2 _____	Conflict situations often 6 _____ if we just wait
Provides a positive 3 _____ for those involved	Loss of face in a conflict situation can damage 7 _____
Difficult due to high levels of 4 _____	
May require training and 5 _____	**Speaker 3**
	The proactive style … 8 _____
Speaker 4	In reality, in most relationships one side 9 _____
It is irresponsible to … 11 _____	Stronger sides … 10 _____
Positive rewards … 12 _____	

2 🎧 10.1 Listen to the debate again and complete the notes. Use the words in the box for answers 1 to 7 and your own words for answers 8 to 12.

> better empathy experience longer lasting
> practice relationships resolve

E Critical thinking

1 Work on your own.

1 Think of a time you dealt with or witnessed someone else dealing with conflict.

2 Make a list of the techniques used. Which were effective? Why?

3 Think about what you learned. What would you advise in a similar situation in the future?

2 Share your experiences and reflections in small groups. Overall, does the group opt for conflict prevention or conflict confrontation?

Study skills | Where next?

The study skills element of this course has provided opportunities to …

- develop an understanding of concepts and skills important for the learning process.
- reflect on your own learning development.
- build your group-work skills.
- develop your planning, prioritization, and self-evaluation skills.

Study skills will remain important throughout your academic and professional life. Success in these domains involves reflecting on the strengths of your knowledge and skills in particular areas relating to studying, and developing your skills through further experience.

One of the first steps to future success in your studies is to identify areas for development and to prioritize these.

© Stella Cottrell (2013)

STUDY SKILLS

1   Work in pairs. Reflect on the study skills covered in the previous units.

   1   Which can you recall now? Review the units to check the others.

   2   Which of the skills have you adopted the most effectively? How? Why?

   3   Which do you plan to use more? Why?

2   Review the table with a partner. Discuss your understanding of each area identified in the fourth column.

Already good	Want to know more	Want to develop further	Knowledge, skills, qualities, and experience	Order of importance
			Understanding success and self-management	
			People skills	
			Creative thinking and problem-solving	
			The art of reflection	
			Successful job application	
			Critical and analytical thinking	
			Improving performance on exams and assignments	
			Improving underlying academic skills	

3   Work alone to complete the first three columns for each area of study skills.

4   Share your table with a partner and discuss the questions.

   1   How similar are your self-assessments?

   2   How important is each area you identified for your future development? Rank them.

   3   What resources will you use to develop the skills you wish to develop in the future?

Role conflicts

A Vocabulary preview

1 Match the words in bold with the correct definitions.

1	**accommodate** (v)	a	when two or more people or things share responsibility for something
2	**compliance** (n)	b	between or among
3	**inter-** (prefix)	c	relating to a group of people who have a particular shared purpose
4	**intra-** (prefix)	d	to do something with only a few people to find out if something will be successful
5	**organizational** (adj)	e	within
6	**overlap** (v)	f	to consider and include something when deciding what to do
7	**pilot** (v)	g	a secondary or subordinate category
8	**subcategory** (n)	h	the practice of obeying a law, rule, or request

2 Complete the sentences using the words in bold from Exercise 1.

1 _____ with the law is what makes society possible.

2 _____ personal skills (understanding other people) are vital when people disagree strongly with each other.

3 _____ personal skills (understanding yourself) help you get along with others.

4 It helps when learning vocabulary to divide it into _____.

5 It is best to _____ a new way of solving problems in a low-stakes situation.

6 Modern workplaces must be flexible enough to _____ different work patterns.

7 _____ efficiency mainly comes from good management.

8 There is an _____ between the roles of teacher and parent.

B Before you listen

1 Think of two lecturers you have had during your academic career. Describe the style and approach of each one to your partner. Use the ideas in the box.

> organization of material   speed of delivery
> style of lecture   visuals and support material provided

2 Discuss the questions with your partner.

1 Which elements of the different styles were more challenging?

2 How did you deal with the challenges?

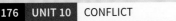

C Global listening

Lecturers may have different styles and adopt a variety of approaches to the delivery of their talks. Identifying the lecturer's style and approach can help you to follow the lecture and take notes more effectively.

If you regularly have the same lecturer, you will become familiar with the speed of delivery, the amount of support provided (e.g., visuals and handouts), and the organization of material. When the lecturer is new to you, be prepared with your notebook and audio recorder. Access all available support material, and listen for clues to the organization of the lecture in the opening to the lecture.

Coping with different lecture styles

1 🎧 10.2 Listen to two parts of a lecture about roles. Identify which lecturer does each thing, Speaker A (Brett Wilson) or Speaker B (Sofia Lang).

1 Provides pre-reading   A / B

2 Starts with examples and then moves to general statements   A / B

3 Encourages interaction   A / B

4 Gives clear verbal signposts for the organization   A / B

5 Speaks faster   A / B

6 Relies on visuals for showing organization   A / B

2 Work in pairs. Identify what is challenging about the techniques from Exercise 1. Discuss ways to deal with them.

D Close listening

1 Review the lecture notes with a partner. Discuss the type of information missing and predict what it could be.

Wilson

Definitions

Role conflict—when a person has [1] _____ one role and it is

[2] _____ to fulfill all of them

– [3] _____ conflict—in organizational context, e.g., a job makes

* incompatible demands*

– [4] _____ conflict— roles in different domains conflict, e.g., family

* vs. [5] _____*

Lang

Example of [6] _____ conflict: mother role vs. academic role

Possible [7] _____ of inter-role conflict:

* Decreasing [8] _____—suggested that women are choosing*

* profession rather than family*

*   → But too complex to [9] _____*

*   → [10] _____ experience the same conflict*

* ∴ cannot say [11] _____ is only women's*

Wilson

Example of [12] _____ conflict: promotion to [13] _____ role,

responsible for meeting management deadlines, but also representing the team

Result—conflict leads to lower [14] _____ and poorer

[15] _____, as shown in several research studies.

Concurrent listening and note-taking

2 🎧 10.2 Listen to the rest of the extracts from the lecture. Complete the notes with one or two words in each blank.

E Critical thinking

1 Identify the roles you have in different areas of your life. Reflect on the following questions.

1 What conflicts have you experienced within or between these roles?

2 What potential conflicts could there be?

3 Does role conflict have a positive side? If so, what? If not, why not?

2 Describe your roles and share your reflections with a partner.

Critical thinking

Making counter arguments and concessions

Making counter arguments and including concessions are effective ways to strengthen your own argument.

By including and dealing with opposing views in the form of counter arguments, you anticipate objections, demonstrate you have considered the issues in depth, and provide strong support for your own conclusions.

A counter argument may highlight a disadvantage of the argument you propose, or give an alternative explanation that seems to make more sense. Such opposing arguments are often introduced with a signpost phrase or question, e.g., *However, it could be said that …, Some people argue that …, Admittedly, …, But isn't this just …?*

To then deal with the counter argument, demonstrate how or why the counter argument is incorrect or how it is less important or probable than your argument. Avoid stating a counter argument without refuting it.

Concessions show respect and consideration for the opposing views, by acknowledging some positive features of them, e.g., *They are correct in the sense that …, While we agree that …*

1   Match the two sets of arguments, counter arguments, and refutations.

The main reason is that women are choosing careers.

Performance doesn't change easily, and studies support the theory of the effect of role conflict.

Fathers face conflict with their roles, so we cannot conclude it is the woman's choice.

The promoted worker's performance went down due to role conflict.

The issue of declining birth rates is too complex to identify one cause.

The promoted worker's performance went down due to laziness.

2   🎧 10.3 Listen to the extracts from the lecture and check your answers to Exercise 1.

3   Work in pairs. Use the ideas below to make an argument.

Having many roles …   Conflict is good when …

Avoiding conflict is …   Roles need to be …

4   With your partner, prepare a counter argument for each statement. Include it in your sentence, together with an attempt to rebut it.

Vocabulary development

Words for describing behavior

1 Match the words from the box with the correct meaning.

> authority   boundary   changeable   constructive
> decisive   delegate   praise   proactive

1 _____ taking action and making changes before they need to be made

2 _____ someone who is considered an expert in a particular subject

3 _____ something that marks where one area begins and another ends

4 _____ tending to change suddenly and often

5 _____ intended to be useful or helpful

6 _____ making the final result of a situation certain

7 _____ to express strong approval or admiration of something or someone

8 _____ to give part of your work or responsibilities to someone

2 Choose the correct words to complete the questions.

1 Is it more important to **praise / delegate** children for good behavior or punish them when they are bad?

2 Are people's personalities ever generally **changeable / authority**?

3 Do you think good managers should **boundary / delegate** a lot or a little?

4 Does being **proactive / delegate** mean you sometimes take risks?

5 How can you give **constructive / decisive** criticism rather than negative criticism?

6 Is it always useful to create a/an **authority / boundary** around your role at work?

7 When people don't agree, is it good to be **praise / decisive**?

8 Why do some people have natural **authority / changeable**?

3 Ask and answer the questions in Exercise 2 with a partner.

Academic words

1 Match the words in bold with the correct definitions.

1 **amend** (v)
2 **incentive** (n)
3 **inherent** (adj)
4 **negate** (v)
5 **radical** (adj)
6 **refine** (v)
7 **unify** (v)
8 **violation** (n)

a to unite people or countries so they will work together
b to make something have no effect
c to make small changes to something in order to improve it
d very different from the usual way
e describing a basic or essential feature that gives something its character
f an action that is in opposition to a law, agreement, principle, etc.
g something that makes you want to do something because you know you will benefit
h to make changes to a document, law, agreement, etc., especially in order to improve it

2 Complete each sentence with a word in bold from Exercise 1.

1 It is a _____ of a worker's rights to expect them to work more than five days a week.
2 It is best to give a/an _____ to young people to help with household chores.
3 Management should explain why if they _____ the rules in any way.
4 One bad decision can easily _____ years of work in government.
5 _____ views are never welcomed in the workplace or college.
6 To _____ a group that is not working well together, you need to talk.
7 You should always _____ your ideas as far as possible before sharing them.
8 It is _____ in the role of a doctor to be discreet.

3 Choose the three sentences you most agree or disagree with in Exercise 2. Explain your choices to a partner.

Speaking model

You are going to learn about using adverbs to modify or expand statements, talking with people with different accents, and the principles and structure of formal debates. You are then going to participate in a debate about conflict.

A Analyze

Read the discussion. Answer the questions.

1 What is the debate motion?
2 Which speaker is for the motion and which is against?
3 What concession is made?

CARL: Good morning, ladies and gentlemen, and welcome to the debate. The motion for today is that conflict between individuals is inevitable and natural. Proposing the motion, we have Kat and Jan. Opposing the motion, we have Sal and Tiana.

I would now like to call on the first speaker of the proposition, Kat, to open the debate.

KAT: Good afternoon, Mr. Chairman, ladies, and gentlemen. The topic for our debate is conflict between individuals being inevitable and natural. We define conflict as any disagreement that makes people unhappy. We as the affirmative team believe that this is true. As first speaker for the motion, I am going to discuss two points. Our second speaker for the motion will rebut and sum up our team's case.

My first argument is that individuals, by definition, are all different. Society makes us live and work together, and it is therefore inevitable that there will be conflict. My second point is that all groups of animals and humans that live together display conflict. A group of lions may reject one of its members in a dispute over leadership. Conflict is inherent in the way groups work together, and it is therefore clearly natural. So, Mr. Chairman, ladies, and gentlemen, in conclusion we should not expect to live in society without sometimes having a conflict.

SAL: Mr. Chairman, ladies, and gentlemen … we agree with the topic and definition given by the first affirmative speaker. However, we believe that the statement is false. As first speaker, I will give you two arguments to show that conflict is not inevitable or natural. Our second speaker will rebut and sum up our team's case. My main point is that, although I agree with the first speaker that many groups do have conflict, there are also many societies or groups that avoid conflict by being proactive. For example, Buddhist priests organize themselves in a way that they all agree with. And my second point is that the motion suggests that natural is good, but that is simply not true. We are part of nature, but we can also change it by changing our behavior.

B Discuss

Discuss the questions in a group. Explain and support your views.

1 What other arguments can you think of for and against the debate motion?
2 What counter arguments can you think of?
3 Without having the debate, which side of the argument do you agree with?

Grammar

Using adverbs to modify statements

Some adverbs can affect the meaning of the entire sentence. These sentence adverbs, often ending in *-ly*, modify the statement as a whole. The adverb expresses the speaker's attitude to what is stated in the sentence.
*It's not, **admittedly**, the easiest method.*

Other adverbs link the sentence to the preceding one.
*But data is not always reliable. **Consequently**, we just don't know for sure.*

1 Complete the extracts from the debate and the lecture with the best adverb.

1 If all the participants at international conferences on world issues like climate change came to the table with this approach, they would, **undoubtedly / consequently**, achieve amazing things.

2 But should we really just give in to anyone who is in conflict with us, even when we know we are right? **Surely / Similarly** it is cowardly to do this.

3 That's when you have roles in two different domains that cannot be easily accommodated, like being a mother and worker, which is, by the way, **fortunately / undoubtedly** the most common example …

4 Professor Lang will start by talking about the work-family dilemma, the inter-role conflict, on which she is **certainly / consequently** one of the most respected authorities.

5 This is a classic example of inter-role conflict … and **hence / actually**, there's nothing radical in this scenario.

6 What actually happened was that he stopped doing the things that got him these jobs in the first place. **Hence / Accordingly**, he ended up doing the minimum required to keep his job.

2 Compare your answers with a partner. Discuss how the adverb modifies the sentence and whether it links it to the previous one.

3 Add a suitable adverb to the statements. More than one may be suitable.

accordingly   basically   certainly   consequently   fortunately
happily   similarly   undoubtedly   unfortunately

1 Conflict is inevitable when people work together.
2 Having several roles can create conflict for the person.
3 Preventing conflict is often the less expensive option. It can be the less stressful option.
4 Many people prefer clearly defined roles.
5 Well-defined roles help people to function effectively. Good employers provide clear job descriptions.

Speaking skill

A debate is a formal oral discussion in which individuals or, more usually, teams present arguments and attempt to counter their opponent's arguments. Participating in debates provides the opportunity to develop high-level skills in reasoning, teamwork, and also public speaking.

Though the basic principles of debates remain the same in different contexts, the format can vary in terms of time allowed for speakers, the order of speakers from the affirmative and negative teams, and how arguments are presented.

Before participating in a debate, your team should be sure of the structure and format being used, e.g.:

- number and order of speakers
- time for each speaker
- appropriate phrases to use at each stage.

1 Match the formal debate phrases (1–10) with the sections of the debate (A–G).

1 As the first speaker, I will be discussing …	A	Introduction
2 Good morning Mr./Madam Chairman, ladies, and gentleman.	B	Definition of topic
3 We wish to argue that …	C	Stating side
4 Mr./Madam Chairman, ladies, and gentleman, in conclusion …	D	Organization of debate
5 My first point is …	E	Arguments
6 Our second speaker will rebut …	F	Rebuttal
7 The topic for our debate is …	G	Ending
8 This can be clearly seen …		
9 We define the topic as …		
10 We, the affirmative team, believe this proposition to be true.		

2 Identify useful debating phrases in the Speaking model.

3 Work in a group of five. Practice the framework of a debate for the following motion: *Conflict between individuals is inevitable and natural.*

1 Decide who has which role.

2 Follow the plan above.

3 Practice the framework. (Use ideas from the Speaking model and/or your own for the arguments.)

4 Change roles.

Pronunciation for speaking

Talking to speakers with different accents

With English as an international language, there are now many more non-native speakers of English than native speakers. When you communicate in English, you will be speaking with people with a range of accents different from your own.

English speakers, both native and non-native, need to focus on intelligibility, that is, how easy they are to understand, rather than having a "perfect" accent. Important features of pronunciation for intelligibility include sentence stress and rhythm, speed of speech, and word stress.

To communicate successfully in English, do the following.

- Develop an awareness of your own English in relation to these key features.
- Ask for feedback from people you speak English with.
- Check that you are being understood when speaking with others.

1 🎧 10.4 Work in pairs. Listen and discuss how easily you understand the accent in each extract, and why.

2 Tell your partner about the different roles you have in your life. When you listen, observe how clear your partner is in the three areas below. Then give feedback.

sentence stress and rhythm
speed of speech
word stress

3 Review the Speaking model. Then work in groups, with each taking one of the roles from the debate. Have the same debate from memory, focusing on clear communication.

Speaking task

Have a debate. The proposition is: *Conflict between communities is inevitable and natural.*

Brainstorm

Review *Conflict resolution* and *Role conflicts* and the Speaking lesson.

Work in pairs to do the following.

- Make a list of arguments to support the proposition.
- Identify a counter argument for each argument.
- Do the same to refute the proposition.
- Confirm with your teacher which side of the debate you will be on.
- Select a total of four arguments to present for your side in the debate.
- Research facts and statistics to support these arguments.

Plan

Decide who will speak first and the order of your arguments. Practice your side of the debate, using expressions for formal debates.

Speak

Have a formal debate with another pair, a chairperson, and an audience. The audience will vote on the winning side at the end.

Share

Share feedback about your experiences of the debate as a debater, chairperson, or audience member.

- What worked well?
- What were the challenges?
- What could be done differently next time?

Reflect

Using the information you learned throughout the unit, answer the questions.

1   What are the benefits of debating?
2   How can people manage their roles most effectively?
3   How far is conflict inevitable and natural?

Review

Wordlist

MACMILLAN DICTIONARY

Vocabulary preview

accommodate (v) *	organizational (adj)	resolution (n) *
compliance (n) *	overlap (v) *	subcategory (n)
conciliation (n)	pilot (v)	theoretical (adj) **
empathy (n)	preventative (adj)	undeniable (adj)
fake (adj)	proposition (n) **	

Vocabulary development

authority (n) ***	constructive (adj) *	praise (v) **
boundary (n) **	decisive (adj) **	proactive (adj)
changeable (adj)	delegate (v) *	

Academic words

amend (v) **	negate (v)	unify (v)
incentive (n) **	radical (adj) **	violation (n) *
inherent (adj) *	refine (v)	

Academic words review

Complete the sentences with the correct form of the words in the box.

amend	marginal	principle	radical	rigid

1 In a _____ departure from his earlier promises, Professor Sayeed decided to retire this year.

2 She resisted me on _____—not because she thought it would work, but due to what she believed in.

3 The main area of research here is medicine. The others are _____ .

4 There's plenty of time to _____ your version of the paper and send it back to us once it's improved.

5 Researchers are less _____ in their methods, more open to experimentation.

Unit review

Listening 1		I can listen and anticipate information to come.
Listening 2		I can cope with different lecture styles.
Study skill		I can decide on next steps in my development.
Vocabulary		I can use words for describing behavior.
Grammar		I can use adverbs to modify statements.
Speaking		I can use the principles and structure of formal debates.

Presentation slides

Listen to the lecture from Unit 3, page 52. Annotate the slides.

4

Sunk-cost fallacy
How Important Is the past?

Should past investment affect choices now?

5

Sunk-cost fallacy
Typlcal behavlor
- Don't like wasting energy and effort
- Continue "investing"

Fallacy
- Original aims often forgotten or changed

6

Sunk-cost fallacy
Business advice
- Give up and walk away

Alternative view
- Reconsider original aims
- They may still be valid

7

Legacy systems
Technological systems
- Effective in the past
- Not good enough for now

8

Legacy systems
Issues with system change
- Cost
- Security
- Data transfer
- Unwillingness

9

Legacy systems
Focus on the outcome
- Avoid sunk-cost fallacy
- Remain competitive

Functional language phrase bank

The phrases below give common ways of expressing useful functions. Use them to help you as you're completing the *Discussion points* and *Developing critical thinking* activities.

Asking for clarification
Sorry, can you explain that some more?
Could you say that another way?
When you say … do you mean …?
Sorry, I don't follow that.
What do you mean?

Asking for repetition
Could you repeat that, please?
I'm sorry, I didn't catch that.
Could you say that again?

When you don't know the word for something
What does … mean?
Sorry, I'm not sure what … means.

Working with a partner
Would you like to start?
Shall I go first?
Shall we do this one first?
Where do you want to begin?

Giving opinions
I think that …
It seems to me that …
In my opinion …
As I see it …

Agreeing and disagreeing
I know what you mean.
That's true.
You have a point there.
Yes. I see what you're saying, but …
I understand your point, but …
I don't think that's true.

Asking for opinions
Do you think …?
Do you feel …?
What do you think about …?

How about you, Jennifer? What do you think?
What about you?
Does anyone have any other ideas?
Do you have any thoughts on this?

Asking for more information
In what way?
Why do you think that?
Can you give an example?

Not giving a strong preference
It doesn't matter to me.
I don't really have a strong preference.
I've never really thought about that.
Either is fine.

Expressing interest
I'd like to hear more about that.
That sounds interesting.
How interesting!
Tell me more about that.

Giving reasons
This is … because …
This has to be … because …
I think … because …

Checking understanding
Do you know what I mean?
Do you see what I'm saying?
Are you following me?

Putting things in order
This needs to come first because …
I think this is the most/least important because …
For me, this is the most/least relevant because …

Academic words revision

Units 1–5

Complete the sentences using the correct form of the words in the box.

criteria   distinction   framework   incompatible
intervention   manipulate   mature

1 The young animals are blue and green; the _____ individuals turn gray and black.

2 The new equipment is _____ with the existing computer system and needs replacing.

3 All entrance tests and essays are marked according to the same set of _____.

4 Ricardo managed to save the whole team with his timely _____ during the debate.

5 Despite being accused of trying to _____ the experiment results, he published the paper.

6 Within the _____ of scientific publications, such creative papers are very unusual.

7 Her work in this area is exemplary and deserves a _____.

Units 6–10

Complete the sentences using the correct form of the words in the box.

arbitrary   consultation   duration   incentive   negate
persistent   sustain

1 We didn't do all this hard work just for you to come and _____ it with one comment!

2 There is now added _____ for freshmen to ride their bikes—free energy drinks at the cafeteria.

3 The rain will become _____ tomorrow, and is unlikely to stop before Saturday.

4 He claims to have thought this through, but I know his choice was _____.

5 After a period of _____, the union decided to implement some of the changes.

6 One ticket entitles you to travel anywhere for the _____ of five hours.

7 I don't think we can _____ this level of spending much longer—cuts are necessary.

Macmillan Education
4 Crinan Street
London N1 9XW
A division of Springer Nature Limited

Companies and representatives throughout the world

ISBN 978-1-380-00599-1

This edition published 2018
First edition entitled "Skillful" published 2012 by Springer Nature Limited

Designed by emc design ltd
Illustrated by emc design ltd
Cover design by emc design ltd
Cover illustration/photograph by Getty Images/Moment Open/Alicia Llop
Picture research by Julie-anne Wilce

The publishers would like to thank the following for their thoughtful insights and perceptive comments during the development of the material: Dalal Al Hitty University of Bahrain, Bahrain; Karin Heuert Galvao, i-Study Interactive Learning, São Paulo, Brazil; Ohanes Sakris Australian College of Kuwait, Kuwait; Eoin Jordan, Xi'an Jiaotong Liverpool University, Suzhou, China; Aaron Rotsinger, Xi'an Jiaotong-Liverpool University, Suzhou, China; Dr. Osman Z. Barnawi, Royal Commission Colleges and Institutes, Yanbu, Saudi Arabia; Andrew Lasher, SUNY Korea, Incheon, South Korea; Fatoş Ugur Eskicirak (Fatoş Uğur Eskiçırak) Bahçeşehir University, Istanbul, Turkey; Dr. Asmaa Awad, University of Sharjah, Sharjah, United Arab Emirates; Amy Holtby, Khalifa University of Science and Technology, Abu Dhabi, United Arab Emirates, Dr. Christina Gitsaki, Zayed University, Dubai, United Arab Emirates.

The author and publishers would like to thank the following for permission to reproduce their images

Alamy/Ivan Chiosea p17(tr), Alamy/Angelo D'Amico p51(br), Alamy/Olaf Doering p139(tr), Alamy/Mira pp134,135(t),(t); **Getty Images**/Barcroft Media pp8,9(t),(t), Getty Images/Blend Images/Hill Street Studios p49(tr), Getty Images/BSIP/AMELIE-BENOIST pp98.99(t),(t), Getty Images/Creativ Studio Heinemann p123(br), Getty Images/Ethan Daniels pp152,153(t),(t), Getty Images/Drazen p157(tr), Getty Images/DOMINIQUE FAGET pp170.171(t),(t), Getty Images/filadendron p175(tr), Getty Images/Hero Images pp31,69,173(tr),(b),(cr), Getty Images/Gary Houlder p177(cr), Getty Images/kasayizgi p103(tr), Getty Images/Kevin Kozicki p137(tr), Getty Images/Anthony Lee p65(b), Getty Images/Kevin Liu pp44,45(t),(t), Getty Images/Leren Lu p67(tr), Getty Images/Daniel Milchev p33(b), Getty Images/Minden Pictures/Chris Newbert pp80,81(t),(t), Getty Images/Aleksandar Nakic p155(tr), Getty Images/NASA p118(l), Getty Images/Nature Picture Library/Jurgen Freund p159(br), Getty Images/PhotoAlto/Jerome Gorin p83(br), Getty Images/Portra Images p11(br), Getty Images/Monty Rakusen p159(cr), Getty Images/Rich Vintage p105(b), Getty Images/Sydney Roberts p85(bl), Getty Images/skynesher p47(tr), Getty Images/Keren Su pp26,27(t),(t), Getty Images/Vincent Starr Photography p29(b), Getty Images/Bernd Vogel p101(tr), Getty Images/Westend61 p15(b), Getty Images/Gordon Wiltsie pp62,63(t),(t), Getty Images/WIN-Initiative pp116,117(t),(t); **Macmillan Publishers Ltd**/BRAND X p87(2), Macmillan Publishers Ltd/Getty p87(3), Macmillan Publishers Ltd/Getty Images/iStockphoto p87(4), Macmillan Publishers Ltd/PhotoDisc p87(5), Macmillan Publishers Ltd/Photospin p87(1); **Shutterstock**/Rawpixel.com p141(tr); **Thomson Reuters** pp8,26,44,62,80,98,116,134,152,170(bl),(bl),(bl),(bl),(bl),(bl),(bl),(bl),(bl),(bl), Thomson Reuters/Courtesy Wyss Institute at Harvard University, Courtesy Octo Telematics, Courtesy TV Globo.

The author(s) and publishers are grateful for permission to reprint the following copyright material: Page 62: Extract from 'Groupthink: the bane of high performing Agile Teams' by Matthew Hodgson. © 2014 Zen Ex Machina Pty Ltd. Reprinted with permission. zenexmachina.com.

Printed and bound in China

2023 2022 2021 2020 2019
15 14 13 12 11 10 9

PALGRAVE STUDY SKILLS

by bestselling author, **Stella Cottrell**

  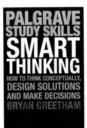   

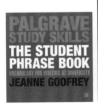   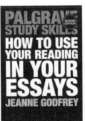  

palgravestudyskills.com

 facebook.com/skills4study

 twitter.com/skills4study